THE
MYTHICAL
CREATURES
BIBLE

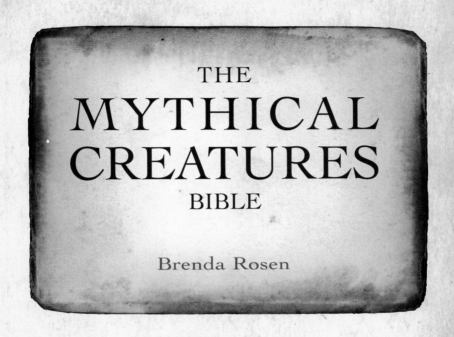

THE
MYTHICAL
CREATURES
BIBLE

Brenda Rosen

THE DEFINITIVE GUIDE TO LEGENDARY BEINGS

STERLING
New York

14 16 18 20 19 17 15 13

First published in the U.S. in 2009 by Sterling Publishing Co., Inc.
1166 Avenue of the Americas, New York, NY 10036

First published in Great Britain in 2008 by Godsfield Press
A division of Octopus Publishing Group Ltd
50 Victoria Embankment, London, EC4Y 0DZ

Distributed in Canada by Sterling Publishing Co., Inc.
C/o Canadian Manda Group. 664 Annette Street
Toronto, Ontario, Canada M6S 2C8

For information about custom editions, special sales, premium
and corporate purchases, please contact Sterling Special Sales
Department at 800-805-5489 or
specialsales@sterlingpublishing.com.

Manufactured in China

ISBN 978-1-4027-6536-0

Cover Illustrations: © Octopus Publishing Group
Limited/Dean Spencer, John Higgins, Nick Harris,
David Bergen, Rhian Nest James, Jane Evans.

Contents

PART ONE

Introduction

What are mythical creatures?

THE LEGENDS, FOLKTALES, AND SPIRITUAL STORIES OF PEOPLES
AROUND THE WORLD HAVE ALWAYS BEEN FILLED WITH MYTHICAL
CREATURES. FROM THE EARLIEST TALES TOLD AROUND THE FIRE TO
THE BOOKS AND MOVIES THAT DELIGHT AND TERRIFY US TODAY, THE
HUMAN IMAGINATION HAS POPULATED THE WORLD WITH A
MARVELOUS VARIETY OF MAGICAL AND MENACING ANIMALS,
MONSTERS, SPIRITS, AND GODS.

Some of the fabulous creatures of storytelling and legend appear in multiple traditions. Dragons and other winged serpents, for instance, appear in the legends of virtually every culture, from ancient Egypt, Babylonia, India, and China, to medieval Europe and Mesoamerica (the area where a number of pre-Columbian societies flourished before the Spanish arrived). Other creatures reflect the concerns of particular geography, such as the Mermaids that swim through the stories of sea-going peoples from Melanesia, to Japan through to the British Isles. Terrifying giants, Zombies, and Vampires have haunted world folklore from ancient times to today.

Real and imagined

Accounts sent home by early travelers, explorers and traders are filled with fabulous creatures. Some were probably garbled descriptions of real animals, such as the Camelopard, which ancient Romans described as having the proportions of a camel, the spotted skin of a leopard and two backward-curving horns—a description that seems to fit a real giraffe. Others are likely fanciful exaggerations aimed at elevating the teller's reputation, and include the fanciful Sirens and sea monsters of sailors' stories or the giant wolves and magical stags stalked by hunters in European folktales.

In many spiritual traditions, the gods appear in animal form. In ancient Egypt, the goddess Hathor, who personifies the Milky Way, has the head of a cow, while Anubis, the god of the dead, is jackal-headed. Sacred animals are also divine helpers. The winged steed Buraq carries the Prophet Muhammad on his miraculous journey. Creation stories include many marvelous creatures, from the devilish snake of Genesis to the giant turtle that supports the Earth in Native American legend. Often, in these creation myths the world is brought into being when a hero slays a supernatural creature, such as the monster Tiamat from whose corpse the Babylonian hero Marduk fashions Heaven and Earth.

Persian Dragon

Why learn about mythical creatures?

ALMOST ALL OF THE CREATURES IN THIS BOOK WERE BORN FROM
THE EXPERIENCES OF OUR ANCESTORS, OUR MANY-TIMES-GREAT
GRANDMOTHERS AND GRANDFATHERS. AS YOU READ ABOUT THE
CREATURES THAT DELIGHTED AND FRIGHTENED THE PEOPLE OF THE
PAST, YOU COME TO UNDERSTAND MORE ABOUT THE HUMAN FAMILY
OF WHICH YOU ARE A PART. IN ADDITION, MOST MYTHICAL CREATURES
REFLECT THE WORLD VIEW OF A PARTICULAR COUNTRY OR CULTURE.

It is a mistake, however, to associate the creatures in this book only with ancient history. The marvelous beings that pervade today's fantasy novels and manga comics, role-playing video games, TV shows, and popular movies, are modelled closely on the creatures of traditional mythology and folklore. The creatures you find here can help you explore the roots of these contemporary myths and inspire your own artwork, stories, and projects.

A reflection of nature

Moreover, the astonishing variety of mythical creatures reflects the riotous fecundity of nature. In these days when animal species and indigenous cultures on every continent are threatened with extinction, exploring the wealth of creatures imagined by cultures around the world deepens our connection to the natural world and strengthens our commitment to diversity and an abundant ecological future.

Mythic creatures can also help you to understand yourself. Fabulous creatures are often symbolic of human traits, both our divine qualities and the shadowy parts that we despise and fear. For this reason, imaginary beings fill our dreams and haunt our nightmares, carrying messages from our inner world. This book can help you

Unicorn

understand and interpret these symbols, opening new windows of insight.

Finally, reading the tales of the gods, semi-divine heroes and heroines, nature spirits, and supernatural beings that are told in every culture can rekindle your sense of wonder and deepen your faith. Like the frog that becomes a prince, mythic tales can inspire your own quest for personal and spiritual transformation.

Folktales, legends, and myths

MANY OF THE CREATURES DESCRIBED IN THIS BOOK ARE DRAWN FROM
THE WORLD'S FOLKTALES, LEGENDS, AND MYTHS. IN MANY CASES,
THESE TRADITIONAL STORIES AROSE FROM ATTEMPTS BY EARLY PEOPLES
TO UNDERSTAND AND EXPLAIN THE NATURAL AND SPIRITUAL WORLD.
GENERALLY, THE NARRATIVES EXISTED AS PART OF A CULTURE'S
STORYTELLING TRADITION BEFORE THEY WERE WRITTEN DOWN.

Folktales

These are, as the name implies, stories told
by the folk. In cultures around the world,
folktales are told about animals and other
creatures that talk and behave just as
humans do. Sometimes these tales teach a
moral lesson, such as the fable about the
race won by the slow but steady turtle over
the speedy but over-confident hare. Fairy
tales, a type of folktale, often feature
mythical creatures, such as Fairies, Trolls,
Witches, Giants, Elves, and talking animals.

Legends

Traditional stories that seem to be plausibly
historical, legends often include miraculous
happenings and supernatural beings. One of

Pan Gu

the legends surrounding King Arthur's knights centers on the hunt for the Questing Beast, a monster with the head and neck of a serpent, the body of a leopard, the haunches of a lion, and the hooves of a stag. Legends often celebrate the exploits of a hero, such as the triumphs of Hercules over mythical creatures like Hydra, a many-headed sea serpent.

Hydra

Myths

Stories that feature divine or semi-divine beings are myths. They are the most overtly "religious" type of traditional story and are generally tied closely to a culture's world view and beliefs. Myths can explain the origins of the universe, such as the Chinese story of Pan Gu, the giant who separated the Earth and sky; they can recount epic battles, such as that between the demon Ravana and the hero Rama and his monkey allies in the Hindu *Ramayana*, the ancient Sanskrit epic text. Myths can also explain the origins of a tradition: for instance, the Aztec calendar, said to have been invented by Quetzalcoatl, the Mesoamerican feathered serpent.

Sacred and magical creatures

MANY OF THE MYTHICAL CREATURES EXPLORED HERE HAVE
SUPERNATURAL OR MAGICAL ABILITIES. MORE POWERFUL THAN MERE
HUMANS, BUT LESS POTENT THAN THE SUPREME DEITIES WORSHIPPED
IN THE WORLD'S FAITHS, THESE BEINGS OFTEN BRIDGE THE GAP
BETWEEN RELIGION AND FOLK BELIEFS. SOME CREATURES ARE
GENERALLY BENEFICENT; OTHERS ARE MISCHIEVOUS OR OVERTLY
MALICIOUS. ALL REVEAL SOMETHING SIGNIFICANT ABOUT THE HEARTS
AND MINDS OF THE PEOPLE WHO TELL STORIES ABOUT THEM.

Natural elements

One broad grouping of sacred and magical
creatures consists of beings that personify or
control some aspect of the natural world. In
Greek mythology, each tree and grove was
under the protection of a female nature spirit
called a Dryad. In Mesoamerican beliefs,
important agricultural forces such as the
winds, rain, thunder, and lightning were
honored in deified form. In Egyptian
mythology, Heket, the goddess of fertility
and childbirth, has the head of a frog,
presumably because of the millions of frogs
spawned each year after the flooding of the
Nile. In Japan there is a folk belief that

Boggart

earthquakes are caused by the underground movements of a Dragon-headed beetle called Jinshin-Mushi.

Troublesome forces

Another broad grouping consists of creatures that are troublesome or destructive. Some are personifications of evil forces, such as Rangda, the child-eating demon queen in Balinese mythology. Others are Giants or monsters, either humanoid beings such as Ogres, Gorgons, and Zombies, or animal forms, such as the Kludde, a shape-shifted monster from the folk traditions of Belgium that can appear as a large black dog with leathery wings, or as a bat, raven, or cat. Troublesome or mischievous creatures include household pests, such as the British Boggart who might cause you to misplace your keys, as well as trickster spirits, such as the Native American Coyote, whose pranks upset the usual order to help people break through to fresh ways of thinking.

Wood Nymph

Classical sources

IN ANCIENT GREECE AND ROME, THE BOUNDARIES BETWEEN THE
SPIRITUAL AND MATERIAL WORLDS WERE LESS DEFINED THAN THEY ARE
TODAY. THE GODS WERE LIKE HUMANS, BOTH WERE LIKE ANIMALS AND
PLANTS, AND COMBINATIONS AND TRANSFORMATIONS BETWEEN
CATEGORIES WERE CONSIDERED COMMONPLACE.

Thus in various interconnected tales, Zeus, the king of the gods, transforms himself into a bull to abduct a human woman, a monstrous combination between bull and man called the Minotaur is imprisoned in a maze in Crete, and the semi-divine Greek hero Hercules strangles a giant bull that is ravaging the countryside as one of his 12 labors.

Aristotle's legacy

The Greek philosopher Aristotle (384–322 BCE), considered to be the first natural historian, devoted a large part of his scientific work to sorting out these categories. A meticulous observer, Aristotle described more than 500 animal species and arranged them into categories and hierarchies. He was the first to notice, for example, that dolphins gave birth to live young. For this reason, he correctly classified them with mammals like the beasts of the field, rather than with fish. Less careful observers, who often included mythological and fabulous animals in their zoological works, are nevertheless indebted to Aristotle for establishing a methodology for describing the natural world.

Herodotus' accounts

Another early Greek noted for his observations was Herodotus (c.484–425 BCE), often called the father of history. A tireless traveler, Herodotus visited all parts of Greece and Asia Minor as well as Persia, Babylonia, Palestine and Egypt, collecting

Theseus slaying the
Minotaur.

Basilisk

information for his great work *The Histories*. In addition to his descriptions of places and events, Herodotus includes information about the natural world, including accounts of many fabulous animals—some based on first-hand observation, such as the crocodiles he saw in the Nile, and others that were described to him, such as the Phoenix of Heliopolis and the flying serpents of Arabia. Though Herodotus is sometimes criticized for mixing the incredible with the real, his method was to report faithfully what he had been told on his travels, allowing the reader to decide how much to believe.

Pliny's contributions

Standing on the shoulders of these giants was one of the less careful observers of nature, the Roman natural philosopher Pliny (23–79 CE). His great work *Naturalis Historia* is a massive encyclopedia of ancient knowledge. Drawing on the work of more than a hundred previous writers including

Aristotle, Pliny's volumes are an entertaining blend of science, exaggeration, and fanciful stories. Despite or perhaps because of this mix, Pliny's work became a standard source for classical knowledge about the natural world. Book eight of Pliny's encyclopedia, for example, is devoted to land animals. In addition to the crocodile, camel, and hippopotamus, Pliny includes information about legendary animals such as the Manticore, Basilisk, and Werewolf.

Illustration from Caxton's 1484 edition of *Aesop's Fables*.

Aesop's Fables

Literary collections from Greece and Rome are also widely influential sources of information about mythic creatures. Aesop, a Greek slave and storyteller who lived in the mid-6th century BCE, is credited with a collection of short folktales about personified animals. William Caxton, who printed the first books in English, published a version of *Aesop's Fables* in 1484. The first Chinese translation was made in 1625, after the tales were carried orally to China by a Belgian Jesuit missionary. Aesop's animal characters, including the industrious ant and the lazy grasshopper, the town mouse and the country mouse, and the wolf in sheep's clothing are known today throughout the world.

Ovid's tales

The *Metamorphoses*, a compilation of Roman and Greek mythology by the Latin poet Ovid (43 BCE–17 CE), is among the most widely influential classical works. Ovid's tales of transformation—or metamorphosis —include accounts of many fabulous creatures, including the transformations of gods and humans into spiders, bears, bulls, birds, wolves, and other creatures.

Cultural epics

ANOTHER IMPORTANT SOURCE OF INFORMATION ABOUT MYTHICAL
CREATURES IS THE CULTURAL EPIC. AN EPIC TELLS THE STORY OF THE
LIFE AND DEEDS OF A HERO OR GROUP OF HEROIC CHARACTERS.
OFTEN EXPRESSED IN ELEVATED POETIC LANGUAGE AND CONSISTING
OF A SERIES OF INTERLINKED EPISODES, THE FIRST EPICS WERE SPOKEN
OR SUNG RATHER THAN WRITTEN DOWN AND READ.

Though some epics are attributed to an author, almost all are based on older mythological and oral traditions, and some were not written down until centuries after their composition. Cultural epics express the spirit of a particular national, ethnic, or religious group and relate significant events in the group's origins and history.

The hero of an epic is often superhuman and his deeds, which require great courage or valor, have legendary significance. An epic's setting is vast, sometimes encompassing the known world of the time, and extending in many cases to the heavenly realms and the Underworld. Most important for the transmission of information about mythical creatures, epics generally include supernatural characters, such as gods, angels, and monsters, who interest themselves in the action and often play important roles in the story.

Ancient epics

The earliest known epic, the story of Gilgamesh, dates back to the 3rd millennium BCE. Gilgamesh was a king of ancient Sumeria. The most complete version of his exploits was preserved on 12 clay tablets in the library of a 7th-century BCE Assyrian king. Among the episodes is a battle in which Gilgamesh and his companion slay the Humbaba, the monstrous giant who guards the cedar forest where the gods live. The monster has

Humbaba

the legs of a lion, a vulture's talons, a bull's horns, and a tail that ends in a snake's head. This hybrid combination of parts establishes a pattern that is echoed in many later mythological monsters.

Indian epic

Another early and influential epic comes from the Hindu tradition. The *Ramayana*, attributed to Valmiki and dated from the 4th to the 2nd centuries BCE, presents the teachings of ancient Hindu sages in narrative form. It tells the story of Rama, an avatar or human incarnation of the god Vishnu, whose wife Sita, an avatar of the goddess Lakshmi, is abducted by Ravana, a man-eating demon or rakshasa with ten heads and 20 arms. After an epic battle, Rama rescues Sita with the help of the noble Hanuman, an ape-like creature or vanara who is an avatar of the god Shiva. Here, as in later epics, some mythic creatures are helpful while others are demonic.

Mythic characters from other important ancient epics, including the Babylonian epic of creation the *Enuma Elish*, the Greek epics the *Odyssey* written by Homer, and the

Labors of Hercules, a lost epic attributed to Peisandros of Rhodes, are described later in the book.

Medieval epics

Many of the best-known mythic characters are drawn from retellings of Anglo-Saxon, Norse, and Germanic epics. The earliest of these, *Beowulf*, was composed between 700–750 CE, traditionally in East Anglia, Britain. In the poem, Beowulf, a hero of the Geats (a North Germanic tribe), battles three great mythic antagonists— the swamp-dwelling monster Grendel, Grendel's even more monstrous mother, and later in life, a Dragon that mortally wounds him.

Dragons and other magical beings also appear in Norse and Germanic epics, including the *Eddas* and the *Volsunga* saga, collections of Old Norse legends written down in Iceland in the 13th century, and the *Neibelungenlied*, a 12th-

century German epic. Dwarves, Elves, Giants, and mythic beasts such as the gigantic wolf Fenris and the sea serpent Jörmungandr, as well as numerous gods and goddesses, play important roles in these interlinked tales.

Jörmungandr

Bestiaries

BESTIARIES, POPULAR IN ENGLAND AND FRANCE DURING THE 12TH
CENTURY, WERE ILLUSTRATED VOLUMES THAT DESCRIBED VARIOUS
ANIMALS, BOTH REAL AND IMAGINARY. GENERALLY, EACH ANIMAL
WAS ACCOMPANIED BY A MORAL LESSON. CARVINGS OF BESTIARY
CREATURES ADORN MANY EUROPEAN CHURCHES, AND PRIESTS
FREQUENTLY USED THEM IN THEIR SERMONS TO ILLUSTRATE
THEOLOGICAL IDEAS. FOR INSTANCE, THE PHOENIX, THE BIRD
THAT RISES FROM THE ASHES OF ITS FUNERAL PYRE ON THE THIRD
DAY, WAS OFTEN CITED AS AN EXAMPLE OF CHRIST'S RESURRECTION.

Greek source

The source of information for many
medieval bestiaries was a book of
descriptions of real and fabulous animals,
birds, and other creatures written in Greek
by an unknown author probably during the
2nd century CE. Composed in Alexandria, a
city known at the time for its outstanding
library, the text, entitled the *Physiologus*,
draws on many earlier authorities, including
Aristotle, Herodotus and Pliny.

The author introduces his descriptions of
the animals with the phrase "the physiologus
says." *Physiologus*, which means "naturalist,"
was misunderstood later as being the name
of the author of the book. Many references
to the *Physiologus* in Greek and Latin
writings of the Middle Ages show that the
volume was widely known. Translated into
Latin in around 400 CE, over the next 1,000
years the *Physiologus* was translated and
adapted into almost all of the languages of
Western Europe, inspiring many bestiaries.

Beastly bestiaries

One of the best-known examples is the
Aberdeen Bestiary, a beautifully illuminated
volume whose recorded history can be

Illustration of a Yale from the *Aberdeen Bestiary*.

traced back to 1542 and the library of the Tudor king, Henry VIII. The luxurious illustrations in the manuscript, which scholars believe were created by a single artist, suggest that the volume had been commissioned by a wealthy patron, probably in the 12th century. Each illustration is set in a frame against a background of burnished gold. The colors are rich and bold, featuring reds and blues and the text accompanying each illustration begins with a lavishly decorated initial capital.

Heraldic creatures

BECAUSE HERALDRY CAME INTO USE AT THE TIME BESTIARIES WERE POPULAR, MANY COATS OF ARMS USE MYTHIC CREATURES AS CHARGES (FIGURES PLACED ON THE CENTRAL SHIELD), OR SUPPORTERS (FIGURES PLACED ON EITHER SIDE OF THE SHIELD AND PICTURED AS HOLDING IT UP).

Heraldry, the practice of displaying coats of arms, arose in Europe during the 12th century as a way of distinguishing combating participants whose faces were concealed by helmets. Later, coats of arms were used as wax seals placed on documents, carvings on family tombs and on stained glass windows, banners, and other decorations.

Griffin

Animal symbols

The most popular real animals for coats of arms were the lion and the eagle. The lion, often shown rampant, standing on the left hind foot, symbolized the deathless courage of the person bearing the arms. Eagles, almost always shown with their wings spread, signified that the bearer was a man of action and ingenuity and that he had a lofty spirit, quick understanding, and excellent judgment. The boar, leopard, and bear signalled valor in battle. Among the most popular mythical creatures in heraldry were the Unicorn, Griffin, and Dragon. Their meanings are shown in the table.

Heraldic animals and their meanings

Mythical creature	Heraldic appearance	Meaning
Unicorn	Head and body of a horse, tail of a lion, legs of a stag, with a horn on its forehead	Extreme courage, virtue, and strength
Griffin	Body of a lion, an eagle's head, wings, and talons	Death-defying bravery in battle
Dragon	Giant reptile with scales and forked tongue, eagle's feet, bat's wings, and a barbed tail	Power, protection and wisdom
Cockatrice	Yellow body and wings of a dragon, cockerel's head, neck, and legs	Terror to all beholders
Sphinx	Body of a lion, wings, human face	Omniscience and secrecy
Pegasus	Winged horse	Genius and inspiration
Harpy	Body of a lion, woman's face, neck, and breasts	Fierce when provoked
Mermaid	Woman above the waist, fish below	Eloquence in speech
Centaur	Body of a horse, head and torso of a man	Eminence in the field of battle
Hydra	Dragon with seven heads	Conquest of a powerful enemy
Phoenix	Eagle rising from flames	Long life, miraculous recovery from a deathly wound

Travelers' tales

OTHER SOURCES OF INFORMATION ABOUT MYTHICAL CREATURES
WERE THE REPORTS OF EARLY EXPLORERS AND TRAVELERS. AS A
CONSEQUENCE OF THEIR JOURNEYS THROUGH ASIA AND THE INDIAN
SUB-CONTINENT, MANY NEW AND EXOTIC CREATURES WERE ADDED
TO AN ALREADY LARGE PANTHEON OF REAL AND IMAGINED ANIMALS.

Marco Polo

Born into a family of Venetian traders, Marco Polo (1254–1324) was one of the first Europeans to travel the Silk Road to China. His journey through Asia lasted for 24 years. On his return to Venice in 1295, Marco Polo, who was an engaging storyteller, composed an account of his adventures titled *Il Milione* (*The Million*). The name was probably drawn from the family nickname Emilione, but doubters said that it referred to the book's "million lies." Among the creatures described in the book are monstrous birds that dropped elephants from a height and devoured their carcasses, and a breed of Unicorn-like horses descended from Bucephalus, the legendary mount of Alexander the Great.

Sir John Mandeville

Sir John Mandeville is the name claimed by a supposed English knight who compiled a travel book in Anglo-Norman French, which was published between 1357 and 1371. One of the most popular books of the late Middle Ages, it was translated into many languages. Despite the fantastic nature of its contents, the book was used as a reference by other explorers including Christopher Columbus.

Mandeville describes islands inhabited by creatures with human bodies and the heads of dogs. These beings, called Cynocephali (see pages 102–103), are articulate and social beings, whose king wears an enormous ruby around his neck. Cynocephali are also described by Marco

Illustration from the *Travels of Marco Polo, c.*1412.

Polo, who places them on an island east of Ceylon. Mandeville also describes people whose only source of nourishment was the smell of apples and a people the size of pygmies whose mouths were so small they had to suck their food through reed straws. In India, he claims to have seen cotton plants with tiny lambs growing at the end of their branches. In a nearby country, he saw two-headed wild geese and white-colored lions as large as oxen. In Baçharia, he saw a Griffin with the upper body of an eagle and the lower body of a lion strong enough to seize two oxen yoked together at the plow and carry them to its nest to devour.

Astrological creatures

THE WORD "ZODIAC" COMES FROM GREEK AND MEANS "CIRCLE OF
ANIMALS." WHEN THE ANCIENTS LOOKED AT THE HEAVENS, THEY SAW
THE STARS AS A FIXED BACKGROUND——A RING OF ANIMAL-SHAPED
CONSTELLATIONS——THROUGH WHICH IT LOOKED AS IF THE SUN
PASSED AS IT CIRCLED AROUND THE EARTH.

Zodiac myths

Some historians believe that the practice of using the position of the Sun, Moon, and planets relative to this ring of stars to predict the future originated in Mesopotamia around the 3rd millennium BCE. Priests in Sumeria, Babylonia, and Assyria associated the constellations and planets with their gods. In Babylonia, the planet Jupiter was Marduk, patron deity of the city of Babylon; Venus was Ishtar, the goddess of fertility, sexual love, and war. Correlations between the positions of heavenly bodies and events such as famine and war revealed, the priests said, the will and intention of the gods.

Over the next millennia, the great civilizations of Greece and Egypt elaborated on the theory of astrology and mixed elements of their own mythology with the zodiac signs. For this reason, the myths connected to the signs of the zodiac come from many sources.

Origin of the signs

Aries, the sign of the ram, entered the zodiac from Egyptian lore. Taurus, the bull, came originally from Babylon, where the bull was sacred to Marduk. The Greeks associated the bull with the story of Europa, the Phoenician princess kidnapped by Zeus, the king of the gods who transformed himself into a giant white bull and carried the girl across the sea to Crete. Capricorn, the goat with a fish tail, also came from Babylon, where the god Ea, sometimes called "the antelope of the seas," wore a fish-scale cloak complete with a fish's head and tail. In Greece, Sagittarius was the Centaur Chiron—half-man and half-horse, aiming a bow and arrow—a wise and gentle teacher of hunting, music, and prophecy.

Capricorn

The Chinese zodiac

HISTORIANS BELIEVE THAT ASTROLOGY DEVELOPED IN CHINA
INDEPENDENT OF THE BABYLONIAN / GREEK SYSTEM. THOUGH BOTH
SYSTEMS BREAK TIME INTO 12 DIVISIONS AND ASSOCIATE EACH DIVISION
WITH A MYTHICAL ANIMAL, IN CHINA, THE 12 ANIMALS OF THE ZODIAC
REFER TO A CYCLE OF 12 YEARS RATHER THAN 12 MONTHS.

It seems that animals are a relatively recent addition to Chinese astrology and may have been imported from the shamanic cultures of Tibet and Mongolia, then added to an earlier Chinese calendar sequence called the Twelve Earthly Branches. The association of an animal with each branch made the names of the years easier to remember.

The Chinese animal signs refer to periods of time rather than to constellations. The only Chinese zodiac creature linked to the heavens is the Dragon, a constellation that rises in the eastern sky in the late spring. The symbol of Chinese imperial authority, the Dragon indicates good fortune and great wealth. In Chinese mythology, pearls issue from a Dragon's mouth and gold coins can be found under its feet.

The other animals of the Chinese zodiac are real rather than mythological, but their attributes are personified human qualities. The intelligent Rat, for instance, became the first animal of the zodiac because it tricked the Cat into missing the banquet where the Jade Emperor was to select the zodiac signs; Rat told the Cat that the banquet would take place the following day. Arriving too late to win any place in the calendar, the Cat vowed to be the enemy of the Rat forever. Unlike Western astrology in which the mythical creatures determined the qualities of the zodiac signs, the animals of the Chinese zodiac were assigned to personify the qualities of the signs. For example, the last sign of the zodiac is the comfortable Pig, an ideal symbol of completion and satisfaction.

The Chinese Zodiac

Creatures from film and literature

MYTHICAL CREATURES ARE MORE CENTRAL TO POPULAR CULTURE TODAY THAN THEY HAVE EVER BEEN. BOOKS FROM FINE LITERATURE TO COMIC BOOKS, POPULAR TELEVISION SHOWS AND BLOCKBUSTER MOVIES HAVE DRAWN ON THE FOLKTALES AND MYTHOLOGY OF THE PAST TO DELIGHT AND THRILL AUDIENCES AROUND THE WORLD.

Superheroes

People have always told stories about men and women with abilities beyond those of normal human beings. Extraordinary strength and cunning, enhanced senses, the ability to fly, magical powers of transformation—mythical superheroes from Mesopotamia's Gilgamesh, Greece's Hercules and Odysseus, and China's Eight Immortals and the Monkey King, have used powers like these to enthral people for millennia.

Comic book heroes

Today, American comic book, television, and movie superheroes such as Superman and Spider-Man are widely admired and imitated, inspiring similar

Sun Wukong

characters in other cultures. Japanese *anime* (meaning animation originating from Japan) heroes such as the Super Sentai use magical powers, advanced weapons, and martial arts skills to battle adversaries from other planets and dimensions. In the Philippines, a village girl who swallows a pebble from outer space is transformed into Darna, a mighty warrior whose powers include flight, super strength, speed, and telepathic abilities in a long-running series of popular comic books, television shows, and feature films. Appealing not just to children but also to everyone who feels weak and vulnerable in the face of the world's problems, powerful creatures like these provide popular escapist entertainment.

Monsters

Escape of another kind is provided by monster stories. Monsters appeal not because they are grotesquely inhuman but because they are all too human, embodying qualities that we recognize in ourselves but would sometimes rather disown.

The monster in Mary Shelley's *Frankenstein* (1818) is so hideously ugly that

Frankenstein's monster

he is shunned by everyone, even his own creator, despite his eloquent pleas for friendship and understanding. Though Frankenstein's monster has terrified moviegoers in multiple film adaptations, anyone who has ever suffered rejection can empathize with his rage and pain. The giant gorilla King Kong touches movie audiences in a different way. The monster's tender love scenes with beautiful Ann Darrow, originally portrayed by Fay Wray, draw power from the fairy-tale archetype of *Beauty and the Beast*—in essence a story about the magical and transformative power of love. Space opera villains like *Star Wars'* Darth Vader combine our modern terror of technology gone mad with ancient fears about the evil of which we all are capable. The monster's labored breathing reminds us that everyone who breathes is vulnerable to the seductions of the dark side.

Modern magic

Two of the most successful contemporary fantasy books have strong mythological underpinnings. J.R.R. Tolkien's *The Lord of the Rings* trilogy (1954–1955) has become one of the most popular works of 20th-century literature. Through the wonders of live-action special effects, Tolkien's immense vision has been brought to life in three epic films, all of which are among the most profitable movies of all time.

Tolkien's creation, set in the fictional realm of Middle-earth, draws heavily on Norse and Germanic mythology. Elves, Dwarves, and names such as "Gimli" are Norse. The wizard Gandalf echoes the Germanic deity Odin, sometimes called "the Wanderer" who is often pictured as an old man with long white beard and staff. The magical ring and broken sword of the saga draw on cultural epics such as the Norse *Volsunga* saga and the Germanic *Neibelungenlied*.

A similar worldwide sensation is the series of seven novels by J.K. Rowling about the teenage wizard Harry Potter (1997–2007). Mythical creatures both real and imaginary abound in the novels and film adaptations, including Dragons, Hippogriffs, Unicorns, Centaurs, and a menacing Basilisk, which Harry vanquishes with help from a Phoenix.

King Kong

Cryptozoology

CRYPTOZOOLOGY IS THE SEARCH FOR HIDDEN ANIMALS——CREATURES
THAT HAVE BEEN SEEN BY WITNESSES OR ABOUT WHICH LOCAL
LEGENDS ARE TOLD, BUT WHOSE EXISTENCE HAS NOT BEEN PROVED
CONCLUSIVELY. DRAWING ON SCIENTIFIC RESEARCH AS WELL AS
ON HISTORY, ANTHROPOLOGY, MYTH, AND FOLKLORE,
CRYPTOZOOLOGISTS TRY TO UNCOVER EVIDENCE FOR A WIDE
RANGE OF LEGENDARY AND MYTHICAL CREATURES.

Bigfoot

Just as reports by early travelers and explorers like Marco Polo were dismissed as fabrications, sightings of legendary creatures are often discounted. However, anecdotal evidence for the existence of some legendary creatures is credible if not convincing. Over the past 40 years, for instance, there have been more than 3,000 reported sightings of Bigfoot (or Sasquatch, as it is sometimes called), a giant ape-like creature, mainly in the Pacific Northwest region of the United States (see also page 41). Moreover, supporters of cryptozoology point out that reports of the existence of many unfamiliar animals, including the duck-billed platypus, mountain gorilla, and Komodo dragon, were originally considered to be hoaxes but the creatures were later proved to exist.

Giant squid

A case in point is the giant squid. Tales of many-armed sea monsters large enough to sink ships have been told by mariners since ancient times. Scylla, the monster that threatened the ships of Odysseus in Greek mythology, and the Kraken of Scandinavian lore that was said to be the size of a floating island, are likely early references to the giant squid. In the mid-19th century, evidence mounted for its actual existence.

Kraken

The French gunboat *Alecton* successfully captured part of a squid in 1861. Over the next decades, other specimens washed ashore, mainly in Newfoundland. However, it was not until 2004 that a Japanese team successfully recorded images of a giant squid in its natural habitat. Recent proof of other legendary creatures, such as the megamouth shark in 1976, gives cryptozoologists hope that many mythical creatures will someday be discovered, perhaps with the help of satellite images.

Yeti, Nessie, and Bigfoot

THESE THREE FAMOUS CREATURES HAVE CAPTURED THE IMAGINATION
AND ATTENTION OF CRYPTOZOOLOGISTS FOR SEVERAL CENTURIES—
AND TO DATE NO FIRM EVIDENCE HAS BEEN FOUND TO PROVE THEIR
EXISTENCE. THE LACK OF EVIDENCE HASN'T STOPPED THESE MYTHICAL
CREATURES FROM POPPING UP IN THE MEDIA AND POPULAR CULTURE.

Abominable Snowman

A similar ape-like creature called the Yeti or
Abominable Snowman is said to live in the
Himalayan regions of Tibet, Nepal, and
Bhutan. The first Westerner to find evidence
of the creature was Charles Howard-Bury
who led a Royal Geographical Society
expedition to Mount Everest in 1921. He
saw footprints in the snow on a high
mountain pass that looked like those of a
barefooted man. An Indian newspaper
reporter mistranslated the Tibetan name of
the creature, dubbing it the "Abominable
Snowman." Other climbers and travelers to
the region have made similar reports and
have even photographed the creature's
footprints, but its existence has not yet
been proved.

Loch Ness monster

Equally famous is Nessie, a serpentine
creature roughly 30 feet (9 meters) long,
which is said to inhabit Scotland's Loch Ness.
Some have explained the creature as a
prehistoric Plesiosaur; others say it is a
version of the Kelpie, a Celtic mythological
creature that would emerge from a lake, turn
into a horse, lure a weary traveler on to its
back and gallop into the lake to devour him.
The lack of hard evidence for the existence
of the creature does not deter the busloads of
tourists who descend on the loch hoping for
a glimpse. In 2007, a popular movie called
The Water Horse brought the Loch Ness
legend to a new audience. In it, a young boy
finds an egg and raises the creature in a
bathtub, before releasing it into the loch.

Bigfoot

North American giant

One of the most famous creatures sought by cryptozoologists is Bigfoot, also known as Sasquatch (see page 38). Reports describe the creature as upright and ape-like, between 7 and 10 feet (2 and 3 meters) tall, and covered with dark brown or reddish hair. Bigfoot has been sighted in Washington, Oregon, and the Canadian province of British Columbia since the 1860s. The name "Bigfoot" derives from giant footprints reportedly found by road workers in Humboldt County, California, in 1958. Though many scientists find evidence for the existence of Bigfoot dubious, a number of respected researchers believe that a strong case can be made for the creature.

Using this book

THE CREATURES DESCRIBED IN THIS BOOK COME FROM CULTURES ALL OVER THE WORLD AND FROM ANCIENT TIMES TO THE PRESENT DAY. THE FOLLOWING SECTIONS WILL INTRODUCE YOU TO CREATURES DRAWN FROM LAND, SEA, AIR, AND BEYOND YOUR WILDEST IMAGINATION!

Fabulous animals

Throughout the next section, you'll find information about fabulous animals, including the most famous mythical creatures—Dragons and Unicorns. In addition to these, in the section on land creatures, you will find stories about famous cattle, bulls, and swine; serpent creatures; hybrids—creatures that have parts from two or more animals; and creatures drawn from local legend, similar to those sought by cryptozoologists. Water creatures include mermaids and other merfolk as well as fabulous fish and sea serpents. Air creatures include famous birds, such as the Phoenix, as well as fabulous insects. Similar creatures have been grouped together to facilitate comparisons between cultures and across time.

The Shadow World

In the following section, you'll venture into the Shadow World and read about Werewolves, Vampires, Giants from many lands, and other monstrous beings. Some of the shadow Creatures in the book come

Firebird

from folklore and local legend; others are drawn from mythology and ancient literature. As you read about these terrible creatures, ask yourself what human qualities they embody and why people over the centuries have found them so frightening.

Nature spirits and sacred creatures

In the section on nature spirits, you'll read about Fairies, Elves, Dwarves, and other folkloric beings of the natural world. Finally, in the section on sacred creatures, you'll explore the animal-headed and animal-like gods and goddesses of many lands, from ancient Egypt and the civilizations of the Near East, to Classical Greece and Rome, to the Hindu and Buddhist deities of India, Tibet, Thailand, and Indonesia, to China and Japan, and, finally, to the gods and goddesses of the

Inari

Aztec, Maya, and other Native American peoples. The stories told about these supernatural beings are among the world's oldest sacred tales, but their themes are universal in their spiritual significance.

PART TWO

Fabulous animals

Marvelous creatures

THE CHILD IN EACH OF US REMEMBERS THE ZOO. ESPECIALLY WHEN WE
WERE VERY YOUNG, EACH NEW CREATURE WAS AN ADVENTURE, A TRIP
TO AN EXOTIC NEW LOCALE——THE FROZEN ARCTIC, GREEN JUNGLE,
OR VAST DESERT. THERE WERE CREATURES WITH SPOTS AND STRIPES,
LONG NOSES AND FORKED TONGUES, CREATURES THAT CHATTERED
AND SANG, SOARED AND SLITHERED. AS WE HEARD THEIR STORIES AND
GAZED INTO THEIR EYES, SOME DELIGHTED US AND OTHERS TERRIFIED.

Baku

The next section of this book is like a trip to a mythical zoo. Some of the animals you meet will be marvelous but familiar—Dragons and Unicorns, the fabulous Phoenix, and menacing Minotaur. Others are likely to be entirely strange—the slippery black Ahuizotl from the Aztec lore of Mexico with a human-shaped hand at the end of its tail; the benevolent Baku from Japanese legend that comes when summoned to eat your bad dreams.

Many of the creatures you meet are connected to a story, legend, or myth. The tales weave in and out of each other and wrap back around, like the snake Ouroboros who devours his own tail. Which Greek hero rides Pegasus, the fabulous flying horse—Perseus who kills the terrifying snake-headed Medusa or

Bellerophon who kills the terrifying three-headed Chimera? And what fabulous horses are ridden by the gods and heroes of other lands, like Buraq who carries Islam's Prophet on a tour of Heaven and Hell and Sleipnir, the eight-legged mount of Odin, the Norse chief god?

To make such connections easier to enjoy, the fabulous animals in this section are grouped by type. First, you'll read about the creatures of the land—Dragons and Unicorns from all over the world; cattle, swine, and sheep; snakes and serpents; hybrid creatures; and legendary beasts. Then you'll dive underwater and meet the Mermaids and sea creatures. Finally, you'll soar with the birds and hover with the insects of world myth and lore.

Buraq

Dragons

DRAGONS ARE PERHAPS THE BEST-KNOWN FABULOUS ANIMALS. IN
VARIOUS FORMS, DRAGONS ARE FOUND IN THE MYTHOLOGY AND
FOLKTALES OF CULTURES THROUGHOUT THE WORLD. THE WORD
"DRAGON" COMES FROM THE ANCIENT GREEK WORD *DRAKONTA*,
WHICH MEANS "TO WATCH."

Greek and Roman Dragons

In an early Greek myth, which may have been adopted by the Greeks from Near Eastern sources, a Dragon guarded the Garden of the Hesperides. The garden was sacred to the goddess Hera, wife of Zeus and king of the gods, and was a wedding gift to Zeus and Hera from the Earth goddess Gaia. On one of the trees in the garden grew golden apples, which conferred immortality on anyone who ate them. Coiled around the base of the tree was a serpent-like, hundred-headed, never-sleeping Dragon named Ladon. Images of Ladon guarding the golden apples often appear on painted Greek vases. The Greek hero Hercules killed Ladon to steal the apples as one of his 12 labors (see page 16).

Python

Another Dragon of early Greek myth was Python, a monstrous being with the head and breasts of a woman and the lower body of a Dragon. Python was said to have been born from the slime and mud left on Earth after the Great Flood.

It lived in a cave near Mount Parnassus and guarded the Oracle of Delphi. Apollo, a son of Zeus and the god of light, music, and poetry, slew Python with his bow and arrows and claimed the oracle for himself. Thereafter, the priestess who spoke the words of the oracle was called the Pythia.

To commemorate his victory, Apollo established the Pythian games, a series of competitions in music, poetry and athletics held every four years, similar to the ancient Olympic games.

Dragon-slayer Cadmus

The early Greek culture hero Cadmus was also a Dragon-slayer. After consulting the Oracle of Delphi, Cadmus slew the Dragon guarding the nearby Castalian spring and on

Apollo kills the Dragon Python.

instructions from Athena, daughter of Zeus and goddess of wisdom, sowed the Dragon's teeth in the ground. From them sprang a race of fierce warriors called the Spartoi. Cadmus then threw a precious jewel into their midst, causing the Spartoi to fight each other. The five surviving warriors helped Cadmus build the great city of Thebes. This tale gave rise to the expression "sowing Dragon's teeth," which means doing something that causes disputes to arise.

The Argonauts

A similar story is part of the myth of Jason and the Golden Fleece, told by Apollonius of Rhodes in his epic poem *Argonautica* (early 3rd century BCE). After defeating an army of warriors that sprang from Dragon's teeth (like Cadmus, see above) by throwing a jewel into their midst that caused them to fight amongst themselves, Jason outsmarted the *Drakon Kholkikos* or the Colchian Dragon who guarded the Golden Fleece. Aided by the powerful sorceress Medea who loved him, Jason drugged the Dragon with an herbal potion supplied by Medea and made off with the golden prize.

Roman Dragons

The Roman Dragon is Draco, a winged serpent breathing fire from its flickering tongue. The dragon-shaped constellation Draco in the far northern sky is one of the 48 constellations named by the mathematician and astronomer Ptolemy (90–168 CE), who lived in Roman Egypt. Some say Draco commemorates the Dragon of the Garden of the Hesperides; others that it is the Dragon killed by Cadmus or by Jason (see above). The Roman natural historian Pliny the Elder (23–79 CE) describes the Dragons of Ethiopia and India in his *Naturalis Historia* as living in caves and subterranean lairs and as being large enough to devour an elephant. In medieval bestiaries based on Roman sources, Draco has the ability to fly and to stun victims by dazzling them with its luminescence.

Draco

Dragons of the Near East

Dragons are also important in the mythology and folklore of ancient Babylon and Persia. Marduk, the principal god of the city of Babylon, is said to have created the world by killing the monstrous female Dragon Tiamat (see pages 282–283). As Babylon grew from a small city-state to the capital of a regional empire, mosaics of the striding Dragon sacred to Marduk were used to adorn the city's walls and gates.

Also called a *sirrush*, which roughly translated means "splendor Dragon," the Babylonian Dragon has a slender, scaly body, a serpent's head, the horns of a viper, the front feet of a lion, the hind feet of an eagle, and a poisonous scorpion's tail.

Biblical references

According to the Book of Daniel in the Old Testament, the great king of Babylon Nebuchadnezzar kept a Dragon in the temple of the god Bel. After casting down the idol of Bel, Daniel boasted to Nebuchadnezzar that he could slay the Dragon without a sword or club. With the king's permission, Daniel boiled pitch, fat and hair together, made cakes and fed them to the Dragon. The Dragon ate them and burst open, angering the Babylonians who threw Daniel into a lions' den.

Persian sources

Persian folktales are filled with Dragons that have scaly, serpentine bodies with a ridged underbelly, but no wings, so they cannot fly. However, they breathe fire and are fierce man-eaters. The most famous Persian Dragon, from the *Shah-nama* (*The Book of Kings*), tells of Rustam who encounters a Dragon guarding a desert spring. Rustam's war-horse Rakhsh has to awaken the hero from sleep three times before he is able to catch and kill the Dragon. In another tale, King Faridun transforms himself into a ferocious Dragon to test the courage of his three sons. Because the youngest son Iraj shows the most wisdom and courage, he is named ruler of Persia (now present-day Iran).

Persian dragon

Dragons of the British Isles

The first Anglo-Saxons to land in England around 450 CE marched under a White Dragon banner. Since then, Dragons have woven their way into the folk memories of the British peoples. From the Welsh Dragons of the *Mabinogion* and the Dragons of Arthurian legend, to the great Dragon slain by St. George, the patron saint of England, the British Isles are rich in Dragon lore.

The flag of Wales

The Red Dragon

Dragons have been the symbol of British kings since mythic times. The *Mabinogion*, the cultural epic of Wales, tells the story of the battle between the Red Dragon (in Welsh *Y Draig Goch*) and an invading White Dragon for control of Britain. According to the tale, the pained shrieks of the fighting Dragons caused women to miscarry and crops to fail. British King Lludd consulted his wise brother Llefelys, who advised him to dig a pit at Dinas Emrys in Snowdonia and fill it with mead. When the Dragons drank the mead and fell asleep, Lludd imprisoned them.

Arthurian legends

The story is continued by 9th-century Welsh cleric Nennius in his *Historia Britonum*. Centuries later, King Vortigern tried to build a castle at Dinas Emrys, but each night, the walls collapsed. A boy who grew up to become the wizard Merlin told the king about the Dragons whose battle had continued underground. The Dragons were released and continued their fight, until the Red Dragon triumphed. In his *History of the Kings of Britain*, Geoffrey of Monmouth (c.1100–1155) cites this victory as a prophecy of the coming of King Arthur, also known as Arthur Pendragon—in Welsh *Pen Draig* means "Chief Dragon."

Over the next 1,000 years, many British kings adorned their battle flags with Dragons. The legendary 7th-century king Cadwaladr ap Cadwallon of Gwynedd used the Red Dragon as his standard. Alfred the Great flew the White Dragon when his army defeated the Vikings at the Battle of Edington in 878. King Athelstan fought under the White Dragon at the Battle of Brananburgh in 937, as did Harold II at the Battle of Stamford Bridge in 1066. In 11th-century battles, the king would position himself between his personal flag and the Dragon standard as a rallying point for soldiers. In 1191, Richard the Lionheart carried a Dragon standard to the Third Crusade. Henry V flew the Dragon standard at the Battle of Agincourt in 1415. During the War of the Roses, Henry VII, who claimed Cadwaladr ap Cadwallon as his ancestor, flew the Red Dragon on the Tudor white and green colors, which gave rise to the Welsh flag still flown today.

St. George and the Dragon

The patron saint of England, St. George (c.280–303 CE) was a soldier of the Holy Roman Empire. The famous story of his encounter with a Dragon probably reached England in the 12th century with the return of the Crusaders from the Holy Land. The tale, which seemed to express everything a chivalrous knight should be, inspired the founding of the Order of the Garter in 1348. Shakespeare underscored the importance of the saint to English pride by having his fictional Henry V rally his troops with the cry, "God for Harry, England and St. George" before the Battle of Agincourt.

Dragon-slaying

According to a medieval version in a book of saints' lives called *The Golden Legend* (1483), the townspeople of Silene in Libya were being terrorized by a Dragon who lived in a nearby lake. To appease the Dragon, a sheep and a virgin were sacrificed each day, the virgin chosen by drawing lots. One day, the lot fell to the daughter of the king of Silene. Distraught, the king offered all his wealth and half his kingdom if the princess could be spared, but the townspeople refused. The princess was taken to the lake dressed as a bride.

Hearing this, St. George rode to the rescue. He charged the Dragon on his warhorse and wounded it with his lance. He then asked the princess to throw him her garter, which he placed around the Dragon's neck. Thus tamed, the Dragon followed the princess like a leashed dog to the center of town. The terrified townspeople offered St. George whatever reward he wanted. Before killing the Dragon, George asked only that the king and townspeople become Christians, which they did. On the spot where the Dragon died, the king built a church to the Virgin Mary and St. George, from which a spring flowed that cured all diseases.

St. George and the Dragon

Jörmungandr

Northern European Dragons

Many northern European myths contain references to Dragons. References to Dragons in Germanic mythology often refer to them as "worms," which means "snake or serpent." The word "worm" (or permutations of the word) is used in old northern European languages to imply "Dragon"—in Old English it is *wyrm*, in Old High German it is *wurm* and in Old Norse it is *ormr*.

Norse Dragons

Jörmungandr was one of the offspring of the fire-giant Loki. According to the *Eddas*, Odin, the chief god in Norse mythology, threw Jörmungandr into the great ocean that encircled Midgard, the known and inhabited world. Jörmungandr grew so large that he was able to surround the world and grasp his own tail.

Thor, the Norse god of thunder and war, was the enemy of Jörmungandr. The god fished for Jörmungandr in the world ocean, using a strong line and a large hook. When the serpent-dragon took the bait, Thor pulled him out of the water using so much force that his foot went through the bottom of the boat. Before Thor could kill the beast with his hammer, the giant Ymir cut the line and the serpent sank beneath the waves. Thor's final encounter with Jörmungandr will come at Ragnarök—the end of the world. At that time, Jörmungandr will rise from the ocean and poison the land and sky, causing the sea to lash against the land. Though Thor will succeed in killing the Dragon, he will walk only nine paces before falling dead from the Dragon's poison.

Germanic Dragons

The *Volsunga* saga tells the story of Fafnir. Originally the son of a dwarf king, Fafnir and his brother Regin killed their father to steal his gold. But Fafnir took the gold from his brother and turned into a Dragon to guard his hoard. The mortal hero Sigurd (Siegfried) avenged this deed by plunging his sword into the Dragon's heart. Fafnir and Siegfried are featured characters in Richard Wagner's *Der Ring des Nibelungen*, a four-part opera cycle based on Germanic and Norse mythology.

Chinese Dragons

The Chinese Dragon—in Chinese *lung* or *long*—has a long, scaly serpentine body and neck, legs like a lizard, and talons like an eagle. Its delicate head has whiskers and deer-like horns, and though it rarely has wings, a Chinese Dragon can be carried across the sky by clouds or ride a waterspout into the heavens.

Symbolically, the Chinese Dragon stands for prosperity and good fortune. This association is often represented by a flaming pearl held in the Dragon's mouth or under its chin. Though fierce, Chinese Dragons are thought to be wise and benevolent.

Imperial symbol

Historically, the Dragon was the emblem of the Chinese emperor and stood for power, excellence, nobility and perseverance. Many Chinese people proudly consider themselves to be "descendants of the Dragon" because their first legendary emperor Huang Di (reigned 2679–2598 BCE), is said to have ascended to Heaven as a Dragon. Chinese emperors sat on the Dragon Throne and adorned their robes with embroidered Dragons. During the Qing Dynasty, commoners could be put to death for wearing clothes with Dragon symbols. Yellow or golden Dragons with five claws were especially associated with the emperor. Carvings of Dragons decorate Chinese imperial palaces and tombs in the Forbidden City in Beijing.

Dragon powers

In Chinese folklore, Dragons control rivers, lakes, and the sea and are associated with the weather as a bringer of rain. Each major body of water was under the control of a Dragon king. In pre-modern times, many Chinese villages had temples dedicated to the local Dragon king. In times of drought or flooding, rituals were performed to appease the Dragon. A famous Chinese folktale illustrates the Dragon's power over the weather. When the daughter of the Dragon king of Lake Tung Ting sent a message to her father's court complaining about her husband, her quick-tempered uncle Qian Tang Dragon rushed to her rescue, flooding the cities and countryside and drowning half a million people.

Dragon embroidery on a
Chinese court offiçal's robe.

Chinese Dragon

Types of Chinese dragons

There are several ways of classifying Chinese Dragons. One system categorizes Dragons by their color, others by their tasks. By legend, there are also Nine Sons of Dragon, each with its own personality and duty. The number nine is considered lucky in China because it is the largest possible single digit. The Nine Sons were frequently used to decorate Chinese buildings, vessels, and weapons. For instance, Qiuniu loves music. Its image is frequently carved on the head of stringed instruments. Yazi is bad-tempered, brave, and loves a fight. Its image appears on ancient sword-hilts and battle-axes. Chaofeng is fearless and loves heights. Its image decorates the corners of ancient palace roofs.

Color classification

- Black Dragons symbolize the north and cause storms by battling in the air.
- Blue Dragons symbolize the east and are a sign of the coming of spring.
- Red Dragons symbolize the west and are associated with the pleasures of summer.
- White Dragons symbolize the south and are a sign of death or impending famine.
- Yellow Dragons are secluded and revered. They convey prayers to the gods.

Cosmic tasks classification

- Tianlong ("Heaven Dragon") is the celestial Dragon that pulls the chariots of the gods and guards their palaces.
- Shenlong ("Spirit Dragon") controls the wind and rain and has to be appeased for good weather to prevail.
- Fucanglong ("Dragon of Hidden Treasures") guards precious metals and jewels buried in the earth. When it bursts from the earth to report to Heaven, a volcano is created.
- Dilong ("Earth Dragon") controls the rivers. In the spring, it resides in Heaven and in autumn, under the sea.
- Yinglong ("Winged Dragon") is the powerful servant of Chinese Emperor Huang Di, who was immortalized as a Dragon. In legend, Yinglong stopped the Yellow River from flooding by digging channels with its tail.
- Jiaolong ("Horned Dragon") lives in the sea and controls floods.
- Panlong ("Coiling Dragon") lives in lakes.
- Huanglong ("Yellow Dragon") taught humans how to write and is known for its scholarly knowledge.
- Longwang ("Dragon Kings") are the rulers of the seas in the four directions.

Japanese, Korean, and Vietnamese Dragons

Like the Chinese Dragons, those of Japan, Korea, and Vietnam tend to be benevolent creatures, involved with the lives of humans and in the fate of nations. Some are tied to the elements, and many are linked specifically to water.

Japanese Dragons

The Japanese Dragon Ryu is a slender, scaled, serpent-like creature with a reptile's head topped with antlers. Generally, the feet of Japanese Dragons have three claws rather than four or five as with Chinese Dragons. Like Chinese Dragons, Japanese Dragons are closely linked to water and to the Imperial Court of Japan. Japanese Emperor Hirohito (reigned 1926–1989) believed that his ancestry could be traced back 125 generations to Princess Fruitful Jewel, daughter of a Dragon king.

Although Japanese Dragons are generally benevolent, there are some exceptions. One of the best-known Japanese Dragon myths tells of an evil Dragon called Yamata-no-Orochi (the Serpent of Koshi) with eight heads, eight tails, and eight claws on each foot. One by one, the beast had devoured seven beautiful sisters. The weeping of the eighth sister, sure that she would be the next victim, attracted the attention of the storm god Susanuo, who came to her rescue. The god transformed the girl into a comb, which he placed in his hair. Then he waited for the Dragon near a vat of sake. As each of the Dragon's eight heads dipped into the liquor and got drunk, Susanuo cut it to pieces with his sword.

Korean and Vietnamese Dragons

The Korean Dragon—*yong* in Korean—is a benevolent creature linked to water and agriculture as a bringer of rain and clouds. Ancient Korean texts also describe speaking Dragons that display human emotions such as devotion, kindness and gratitude. A Korean legend tells of King Munmu who prayed on his deathbed to become the Dragon of the East Sea in order to protect Korea.

In Vietnam, Dragons are called *rông* or *long*. Traditionally, the Vietnamese Dragon's powerful, serpent-like body has 12 sections,

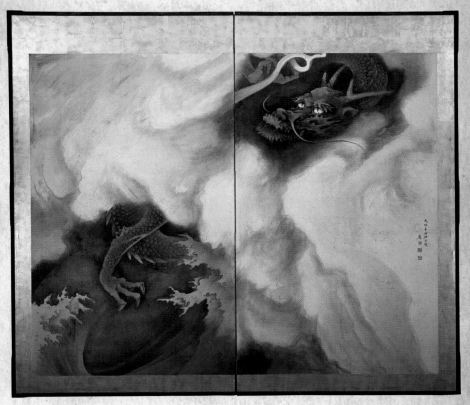

Japanese Dragon screen

symbolizing the 12 months of the year. Vietnamese people trace their ancestry to the marriage between the Dragon Lac Long Quan and the bird-like fairy Au Co, who laid 100 eggs that hatched 100 strong sons. Vietnamese people call themselves Con Rong or "Children of Dragon."

Dragons of Australia and New Zealand

The Dragons of Australia and New Zealand are benevolent creatures. Often living near or associated with water, they are providers of life-giving rains.

The Rainbow Serpent

The Dragon of the Indigenous Australian people is called the Rainbow Serpent. Rock art paintings of the Rainbow Serpent in Arnhem Land in the northeastern corner of the Northern Territory date back more than 6,000 years, making the serpent one of the oldest mythical creatures. Like other serpent-dragons, it is made up of the parts of several animals—the head of a kangaroo or horse, a long snake-like body decorated with water lilies, yams, and waving tendrils, and a pointed or spiked tail like a crocodile.

Folk beliefs connect the Rainbow Serpents to the life-giving fertility of rain. They are said to live in deep waterholes below waterfalls. Rainbow Serpents are also responsible for

Ngalyod (Rainbow Serpent)

storms and floods, which occur to punish people who transgress natural laws. The bones of people swept away in a flood are regurgitated by the Rainbow Serpent and turned into stone. Ceremonies and rituals for fertility and abundance based around the Rainbow Serpent are an important part of Indigenous Australian beliefs and culture. Yingarna is the mother Rainbow Serpent, the original creator being; Ngalyod is the male, the transformer of the land.

The Maori Taniwha

The mythology of the Maori people of New Zealand includes a serpent-like being called the Taniwha. Also an earth-shaper, Taniwha are said to live in deep pools in rivers, dark caves or in the sea. Some can tunnel under the earth, uprooting trees. When they cut channels to the sea, they create harbors. Wellington's harbor is said to have been carved by two Taniwha; the petrified remains of one remains as a hill overlooking the city. At sea, Taniwha can be as large as a whale, but with a lizard or gecko-like shape and a row of spines along the back. Each tribal group has its own Taniwha as a protector.

Unicorns

THE WORD "UNICORN" COMES FROM LATIN—*UNUS* IS "ONE" AND
CORNUS IS "HORN." THE MODERN IMAGE OF THE UNICORN, A
MYSTERIOUSLY BEAUTIFUL HORSE-LIKE CREATURE, BEARDED LIKE A
BILLY-GOAT, WITH A LION'S TAIL, CLOVEN HOOVES, AND A SINGLE
HORN ON ITS FOREHEAD, IS BASED ON ACCOUNTS THAT DATE BACK
TO ANCIENT GREECE AND ROME.

Unicorns in history

To the Greeks, Unicorns were real animals. The earliest description is found in the works of Ctesias, a physician and historian who lived in the 4th century BCE. He described the Unicorn as fleet of foot, with a body like a wild ass but colored white, red, and black and with a horn on its forehead a cubit and a half (30 in./ 72 cm) long. Drinking cups fashioned from the horn, Ctesias wrote, could prevent poisoning.

The Roman natural historian Pliny the Elder elaborated on this picture. He described the Unicorn as having the body of a horse, the head of a stag, the feet of an elephant, the tail of a boar, a deep bellowing voice, and a single black horn two cubits (40 in./96 cm) long.

Unicorn symbolism

In late antiquity, the bestiary attributed to *Physiologus* embellished this description with an allegory explaining the creature's symbolism. Unicorns, it said, can be captured only by a maiden, such as the Virgin Mary. As soon as the Unicorn sees a virgin, it lays its head on her lap and falls asleep, an image that is said to represent Christ's Incarnation. The use of Unicorns in medieval religious art is based on this interpretation.

In the 15th century, Unicorns became popular symbols in heraldry. The Royal

Unicorn

Coat of Arms of the United Kingdom features the lion and the Unicorn as supporters. The lion stands for England; the Unicorn, for Scotland. Traditional rivals, the aggressive lion represents the drive to impose one's ideas of order on the world, while the peaceful Unicorn represents the wish to bring harmony through understanding. Together, they represent an unassailable union of opposites.

The Unicorn tapestries

The height of interest in Unicorns in Europe occurred during the Middle Ages. Thirteenth-century French poet-composers reinterpreted the Unicorn as a symbol of courtly love: the lover is attracted to his lady as the Unicorn is attracted to the maiden. Two remarkable groups of medieval tapestries weave together the courtly and religious themes connected to the Unicorn.

Cluny tapestries

The six tapestries known as *The Lady and the Unicorn* on display at the Musée National du Moyen Age (Cluny Museum) in Paris were woven in around 1460. Against a background of brilliant vermillion sprinkled with flowers is a series of scenes showing a lady and a Unicorn in a lush garden.

Five of the panels illustrate the human senses. To depict sight, for instance, the lady holds a mirror that reflects the image of the Unicorn, which kneels with its front hooves in her lap. For hearing, the Lady plays an organ. For taste, she eats a sweetmeat, and for smell, she weaves a floral crown. For touch, the lady caresses the Unicorn's horn. The sixth panel is more mysterious. Standing in front of a tent with the inscription "To My Sole Desire," the lady places her necklace into a jewelled casket. The lady's gesture may symbolize that she is renouncing the passions aroused by the five senses to seek spiritual fulfillment.

Unicorns at the Met

Another group of tapestries called *The Hunt of the Unicorn*, woven between 1495 and 1505, is displayed in the Metropolitan Museum of Art in New York. Guided by greyhounds, the hunters surround a Unicorn at a fountain, where it is purifying the water by dipping in his horn so that other animals can drink. Though the Unicorn fights fiercely, it is captured and killed when it comes willingly to rest in the lap of a maiden. The Unicorn is carried to the lord and lady of a castle, whose marriage the tapestries may have celebrated. In the final panel, the Unicorn lives again within a walled garden—perhaps a symbol of Christ's Resurrection.

The sense of taste depicted in *The Lady and the Unicorn*.

A Ming Dynasty embroidered silk court official's badge depicting a Ch'i lin Unicorn.

Eastern Unicorns

The Unicorn is also found in Eastern and Middle Eastern mythologies. Certainly, the Chinese Unicorn has a long and venerable tradition and has been a potent symbol in Chinese mythology for 4,000 years. The Unicorn also appears throughout Asia, including Japan and Vietnam.

The Chinese Unicorn

Ch'i lin, the Chinese Unicorn, is a fabulous creature with the body of an antelope, the tail of an ox and a horn 12 feet (3.6 meters) long. It also radiates exquisite colors, has a voice like thousands of wind chimes and walks so softly that its hooves make no sound. A creature of great power and wisdom, Ch'i lin's appearance is a sign of good fortune and signals the birth and sometimes the death of a great leader.

Legends connect the Unicorn with several important Chinese rulers. Toward the end of his life, the legendary sovereign Fu Hsi (c.2852–2738 BCE) is said to have prayed for a way to record his thoughts in order to preserve them for future generations. While he sat on the banks of the Yellow River, Ch'i lin appeared, carrying on its back magical signs that inspired Fu Hsi to invent the eight trigrams that form the basis of Chinese calligraphy. A Unicorn is also said to have walked silently though the palace of Huang Di, the Yellow Emperor, shortly before his death.

Confucius connections

But the most famous Chinese Unicorn legend concerns the birth and death of Confucius (c.551–479 BCE). While on a pilgrimage to a holy shrine to pray for the birth of a son, Ch'i lin appeared to the mother of Confucius and dropped a tiny jade tablet into her hand prophesying the birth of "a throneless king." Though he never ruled as emperor, Confucius had a greater effect on Chinese culture than any monarch. When he was 70 years old and writing his *Spring and Autumn Annals*, Confucius received word that a strange beast had been killed by a hunting party. He recognized the creature immediately as Ch'i lin and began to weep. The last entry in the *Annals* records the death of Ch'i lin, after which the sage lay down his brush for ever.

Japanese Unicorns

The Japanese Unicorns are called Kirin or Sin-you. The Kirin is gentle and solitary, like the Chinese Ch'i lin, while the Sin-you is powerful and fierce, with prominent sinews like a lion and a thick, flowing, tawny lion-like mane. The Sin-you is especially noted for its ability to distinguish right from wrong. According to legend, when the sage Kau You presided in court, he was able to rule effortlessly on questions of guilt or innocence for minor offenses, but when the crime being decided involved a death, he often called upon a Sin-you for guidance. If the accused person was guilty, the Sin-you would fix his eyes on him and pierce him through the heart with its horn.

Vietnam's Unicorn dances

According to Vietnamese folklore, the Unicorn made its first appearance in the land during the Duong Dynasty (c.600 CE). To celebrate the military victory that secured control of the Central Highlands, Emperor Duong Cao To established the annual Unicorn dance to celebrate peace.

Like other Eastern Unicorns, the Vietnamese Unicorn symbolizes happiness, wealth, and prosperity.

During the Tet (New Year's) holiday, Unicorn dances still take place each year. A procession of brightly colored flags leads the procession. After the flags, the Unicorn appears carried aloft by teams of dancers wearing brightly coloured costumes, with drums and cymbals providing a loud, rhythmic accompaniment. The procession visits each home and shop to seek donations to support the festival. The Unicorn dips its heads several times in front of the doorway to encourage the owner. The donation is held out to the Unicorn like bait on a fishing line. Sometimes the gift is suspended in the air and the Unicorn must be elevated on a human pyramid to reach it. With onlookers shouting encouragement, the Unicorn "swallows" the prize. Since the Unicorn symbolizes prosperity, donations to the dance teams are generous.

Gold mythical Japanese Unicorns called Kirin.

Cattle, swine, and sheep

FOUR-LEGGED FABULOUS ANIMALS MAY RESEMBLE THE CATTLE, SWINE,
AND SHEEP WITH WHICH YOU ARE FAMILIAR, BUT THEY ARE ANYTHING
BUT ORDINARY. SOME ARE ENORMOUS, OTHERS CAN CHANGE SHAPE.
STILL OTHERS HAVE POTENT AND DREADFUL
MEANS OF SELF-PROTECTION.

Bonnacon

This wild bull-like mythical animal, also known as the Bonasus, was said to live in the deserts of Asia. First described by Pliny the Elder as inhabiting a country called Paeonia, the beast has the head and body of a bull but the neck and mane of a horse. Its two horns curve inward so that they are useless for defense.

But the Bonnacon has another form of protection. When anyone comes near it, Pliny wrote, it discharges fumes and dung that leave a trail as much as 1,980 feet (604 meters) long. The dung is so hot that it burns trees and sets fire to anything it touches, scorching any pursuers. Illustrations of the creature in medieval bestiaries of the 12th and 13th centuries show hunters in full armor holding up their shields to protect themselves from the noxious blasts.

Catoblepas

This legendary bull-like creature of Ethiopia was first described by Pliny the Elder, and later by the Greek writer Claudius Aelian (c.175–235 CE) in his *On the Nature of Animals*.

According to Aelian, the sluggish and grim creature is about the size of a bull, with a heavy mane that falls over the forehead, narrow blood-shot eyes, a scaly back, and shaggy eyebrows. The beast's head is so heavy that it can only look downward —*catoblepas* is Greek for "that which looks downward."

Catoblepas

This downward gaze is fortunate because the beast's look is poisonous, as is its breath, since it eats only poisonous vegetation. When enemies approach, the beast shudders, glares, bares its teeth, and emits from its throat a blast of foul-smelling breath that causes its enemies to lose their voices and experience fatal convulsions. Knowing this, Aelian says, other animals flee the Catoblepas "as far away as they can."

Gugalanna

Gugalanna is a bull-like creature from the mythology of ancient Sumeria, and is also called Gudanna or the Bull of Heaven. In the *Epic of Gilgamesh*, the hero refuses the attentions of the goddess Ishtar, who has offered to become his lover. Deeply insulted, the goddess begs her father, the sky god Anu, to allow the Bull of Heaven to kill Gilgamesh and destroy his city of Uruk. Anu agrees and Gugalanna comes to Uruk, where it opens caverns in the ground with its breath, sending hundreds of people to their deaths.

Working together again, as they did when they killed the Humbaba (see pages 284–285), Gilgamesh and his friend Enkidu overcome and slay the mighty bull. Ishtar is enraged, but Enkidu insults her, ripping off one of the thighs of the bull and hurling it into her face. For this offense, Enkidu suffers death as the vengeance of the gods.

Mahisha

Mahisha is the buffalo-headed demon defeated by the Hindu warrior goddess Durga. Mahisha was threatening the cosmic order, stomping across the three worlds, polluting the Earth and sea. Though Durga had come into being to defeat Mahisha, in its arrogance the monster sent her a proposal of marriage. "I shall marry only he that defeats me in battle," the goddess replied.

An epic conflict began. Mountains shook and oceans trembled as Mahisha attacked. Armed with Shiva's trident and Vishnu's discus, the goddess battled back. Mahisha changed shape, becoming a lion and then an elephant. But Durga broke the buffalo's horns with her mace, then sheared the lion's mane with her lance, and cut the elephant's trunk with her sword. Finally, she jumped on Mahisha's back, kicking its head with her holy feet. Mahisha fell senseless, and the goddess plunged the trident into its heart. Her victory is celebrated in Bengal each year during the festival of Durgapuja.

The great goddess Durga slaying Mahisha.

Minotaur

The Minotaur, part-man and part-bull, is a creature from Greek mythology. Its story is included in many Greek and Roman source books, including an early encyclopedia of myths and legends entitled the *Bibliotheke* (*Library*), compiled in the 1st and 2nd centuries CE. Minotaur means "bull of Minos," and the most common version of the tale begins with that famous king of Crete.

To prove his worthiness for the throne, Minos prayed to the sea god Poseidon asking him to send a bull as a sign and promising to sacrifice it to the god. In answer, a white bull of unmatched beauty came out of the sea. Presuming that the god would not notice, Minos substituted a lesser bull for the sacrifice and kept the white bull for himself. But Poseidon did notice. Enraged, he caused Pasiphae, the wife of Minos, to become enamoured of the white bull. She engaged the help of the inventor and architect Daedalus, who fashioned a hollow wooden cow in which Pasiphae

Theseus slaying the Minotaur.

could conceal herself to mate with the bull. The result of this union was the Minotaur— a monstrous creature with the body of a man and the head and tail of a bull. As the creature grew, it became ferocious and Daedalus was engaged once again; this time to construct a gigantic labyrinth under the palace to imprison it.

The defeat of the Minotaur

To avenge the death of his son at their hands, King Minos had forced the people of Athens to send seven youths and seven maidens to Crete each year for nine years to be devoured by the Minotaur. In the third year of this pact, the hero Theseus volunteered to be among the victims, promising to try to save them. To comfort his father Aegeus, Theseus promised to return flying a white sail if he succeeded.

When Theseus arrived in Crete, Ariadne, the daughter of King Minos, fell in love with the handsome youth and vowed to help him. Before he was imprisoned in the labyrinth, Ariadne gave him a ball of thread so that he could retrace his steps and escape the maze. Using his strength, cunning, and courage, Theseus killed the monster in a ferocious battle and following the thread, led the Athenian youths out of the labyrinth.

Theseus' neglect

Theseus and the Athenians fled by ship, taking Ariadne with them. When they stopped to rest on the island of Naxos, Theseus abandoned the girl as she lay sleeping. When she awoke, Ariadne was comforted by the god Dionysus, who made her his bride and gave her the constellation Coronis as a marriage garland. But the girl was not the only thing Theseus forgot. He also neglected to change his ship's black sail for a white one. Overcome with grief when he saw the black sail, his father Aegeus leapt off the cliff where he had been watching for his son's return, giving his name to the Aegean Sea.

This wonderful myth has been interpreted in several ways. According to the *Bibliotheke*, the Minotaur's name was Asterion, Greek for "ruler of the stars." Ancient coins from Crete show a labyrinth on one side and the Minotaur surrounded by a circle of stars on the other. Moreover, wall paintings and artifacts unearthed on Crete suggest a cult of bull worship. Thus Pasiphae's union with the white bull can be interpreted as a sacred ceremony, in which the queen as priestess marries the god— perhaps Minos or his priest disguised in a bull's head or mask. The parallel union of Ariadne, also a Cretan priestess, and the god Dionysus supports this interpretation, as does the circle of stars that the god gives her as a marriage garland.

Ancient Greek eye cup with black-figure interior depicting running Minotaur, c.515 BCE.

Khrysomallos

Khrysomallos is a magical flying golden-fleeced ram in Greek mythology. It was born from the union of Poseidon, god of the sea, and the beautiful mortal woman Theophane. To protect Theophane from other suitors, Poseidon transformed her into a beautiful ewe and himself into a ram. From their union, Khrysomallos was born.

When it was grown, Khrysomallos rescued the children Phrixos and Helle as they were about to be sacrificed to Zeus. But Helle fell from the ram as it flew over the sea, giving her name to the Hellespont —the long narrow strait dividing the Balkans from Anatolia (modern Turkey). When he arrived at Colchis, at the far end of the Black Sea, Phrixos sacrificed the ram to Zeus and hung its golden fleece on an oak tree in a sacred grove, where it became the prize sought in the quest of Jason and the Argonauts.

Behemoth

Behemoth is an ox-like creature described in the Book of Job in the Old Testament. Immense and powerful, the Behemoth has a tail like a cedar tree trunk and its bones are like pieces of brass or bars of iron. It lives among the willows of the brook, eats vegetation, and is capable, the Bible says, of drawing up the Jordan River into its mouth. Some say that this description fits the hippopotamus or the sauropod dinosaur, but in Jewish belief, the Behemoth is the primordial creature of the land, as Leviathan is the creature of the sea and Ziz is the creature of the sky. No one can kill a Behemoth except the one who has created it—in this case, the god of the Hebrews. A Jewish legend says that at the end of the world, Leviathan and Behemoth will battle and kill each other, and the righteous people who survive will banquet on the creatures' meat.

Behemoth

Calydonian Boar

In Greek mythology, the Calydonian Boar is an enormous wild boar with a dark bristly coat, a ridge of hair along its spine and deadly tusks.

Because King Oeneus of Calydon had neglected to include Artemis, the goddess of the hunt, in his offering of the first fruits of the harvest, the goddess sent a monstrous wild boar to rampage through the countryside, destroying vineyards and crops with its gleaming tusks, ripping tall trees from the ground, roots and all, and forcing people to seek refuge inside city walls.

Sarcophagus with Calydonian hunt.

Oeneus assembled the greatest heroes of mythic Greece, including Theseus, Jason and some of the Argonauts, Oeneus's son Meleager, and the huntress Atalanta, to hunt the boar. Atalanta drew first blood with an arrow; then Meleager killed the beast with his spear. In love with Atalanta, Meleager tried to award the pelt to her, but his uncles objected to giving the prize to a woman. In the argument that ensued, Meleager killed them.

Twrch Tryth

Twrch Tryth (pronounced "toork trooeeth") is a gigantic boar in the Celtic folklore of Ireland and Wales. Legends say that the

Twrch Tryth

beast was originally a king who was turned into a boar to punish him for his evil deeds.

Because Twrch Tryth, along with its two boar sons, was ravaging the countryside, no less a hero than King Arthur led the hunt against it. Many ferocious battles were fought, and many warriors were gored and slain, until only Twrch Tryth remained.

The Welsh epic *Mabinogion* continues the tale. To win the hand of Olwen, her father demanded that Culhwch, King Arthur's nephew, bring him the comb, shears, and razor from the back of Twrch Tryth to shave him for the wedding. With Arthur's aid, the hunters chased the beast to the top of the cliffs and Culhwch grabbed the magical tokens before the boar leapt into the sea and swam away, never to be seen again.

Serpents

SERPENTS ARE CENTRAL TO THE MYTHOLOGY OF EVERY WORLD
CULTURE. THEY MAY GUARD PRECIOUS SECRETS OR ETERNALLY
DEVOUR THEIR OWN TAILS. SOME ARE FEARFUL MONSTERS; OTHERS
ARE ANCIENT MOTHERS FROM WHOSE BELLIES OTHER MONSTROUS
CREATURES SPRING.

Amphiptere

The Amphiptere is a small winged serpent. Pliny calls the creature a "javelin snake" or Jaculus. Some descriptions say that the creature has two tongues, one serpent-like and the other shaped like an arrow.

According to Arabian mythology, the creature nests in the tops of frankincense trees, which it guards, attracted by the spicy fragrance. When animals or humans come too close to its nest, the creature is said to straighten its body and fly or fall backward from high in the branches, stabbing the animal with its barbed tail. According to legend, many spice hunters have been injured or killed by this attack, which feels like being pierced by a sharp arrow or a hurled javelin.

On medieval coats of arms, the creature often appears wrapped around spears or balanced at the top of poles. The symbol meant "someone who deals justice swiftly." Amphipteres were also carved as stone decorations on English churches.

Amphisbaena

The Amphisbaena is a mythical ant-eating serpent with a head at each end of its body. The name comes from Greek and means "to go both ways." According to Greek mythology, the creature was born from the blood that dripped from the severed head of the snake-haired goddess Medusa (see pages 232–233).

As pictured in medieval bestiaries, the Amphisbaena has two or more scaled,

Amphisbaena

chicken-like feet and feathered wings. Descriptions say that the creature's eyes glow like live coals and that if it is cut in two, the pieces will join together again. It moves by slithering in either direction or by locking its jaws together to roll like a hoop.

Medieval folk beliefs held that wearing a live Amphisbaena around the neck would assure women a healthy pregnancy, that the skin of the creature would cure arthritis and that eating its meat would help a person attract a lover.

Cecrops

Cecrops is a mythical Greek king, a man above the waist, but a snake below. His name is Greek for "face with a tail." Legend says that Cecrops was the first king and founder of the city of Athens and that he taught its people how to read and write and the customs for marriage and burial.

During his reign, the sea god Poseidon and Athena, daughter of Zeus and goddess of wisdom, competed for the right to be the patron deity of Athens. Each was to present the city with a gift, and Cecrops would choose the most worthy. Poseidon struck the rock of the Acropolis with his trident and a spring emerged, but the water was salty. Athena struck the rock with her lance and an olive tree grew on the spot. Since the olive tree brought wood, oil, and food, Cecrops judged it the winner and chose Athena to be the city's patron.

Echidna

In the most ancient layers of Greek mythology, Echidna is known as the "Mother of All Monsters" and her name means "she viper." The early Greek poet Hesiod (c. 700 BCE) described her as immortal and ageless, half-nymph with bright eyes and fair cheeks, and half-snake that strikes swiftly and feeds on living flesh. Her lair is a rocky cave under Mount Etna.

Echidna is usually considered to be the offspring of the union of Tartarus, one of the original forces from which the Cosmos was born, and Gaia, the Earth itself in goddess form. With her mate Typhon, a horrible monster with a hundred snake-like heads, and other partners, Echidna gave birth to many of the most fearful monsters in Greek myth. Her children include Ladon, the hundred-headed dragon, Cerberus, the three-headed dog of Hades, the fearsome Nemean Lion, and hybrid creatures like the Chimera and the Sphinx.

Cecrops

Basilisk and Cockatrice

The Basilisk is a legendary creature of European and Middle Eastern folklore. Over the centuries, the creature's description evolved until it blended with a new creature called the Cockatrice that shared many of its attributes.

In the earliest descriptions, the Basilisk was a small venomous snake with a crown-shaped crest. Because of this crest, the

Basilisk

creature was called the king of reptiles—basilisk comes from Greek and means "little king." Not only was the bite of the Basilisk poisonous, but it could also kill any living thing it touched, breathed on, or even glanced at. The creature was so deadly that trees and grasses in its vicinity were burned up, resulting in the deserts of the Middle East where it lived. In the 1st century CE, Pliny reported that a horseman killed a Basilisk with his lance, but the creature's poison was so strong that it traveled back up the lance and killed both the man and the horse!

Cockatrice

More deadly and powerful

In bestiaries of the 11th and 12th centuries, the creature had grown much larger and its killing powers had evolved to include fiery breath and the ability to kill with the sound of its voice. Medieval travelers were advised to carry protective devices such as a crystal globe to reflect the creature's deadly glance back to it; a weasel, said to be the creature's enemy; or a cockerel because its crowing caused the Basilisk to have a deathly fit.

The Cockatrice emerges

In the 14th century, English author Geoffrey Chaucer mentioned the Basilisk in his *Canterbury Tales*, calling it a "Basilicok," which evolved into the Cockatrice. This new creature combined the original serpent-like Basilisk with the head, neck, and legs of a cockerel. In some descriptions, the new beast also had Dragon-like wings and a human face. As deadly as the Basilisk, the Cockatrice could also rot the fruit off trees and turn people to stone with a look.

Naga

Nagas are large, intelligent, snake-like creatures in Hindu and Buddhist mythology and folklore. Sometimes they are described as being human from the waist up and serpents from the waist down; other depictions give them seven heads and a variety of colors.

In the Hindu epic the *Mahabharata*, Nagas are sometimes venomous persecutors of other creatures and other times act as beneficent helpers. Some take on human appearance. For instance, the Naga King Vasuki helps the gods recover *amrita*, the elixir of immortality, from the Ocean of Milk. The Naga wraps itself around Mount Mandara, which serves as a pivot. Pulled back and forth, the snake churns up *amrita* from the depths of the ocean.

Nagas at Angkor Wat

Carved stone Nagas are guardian figures at many Hindu temples in India and Southeast Asia. Balustrades in the shape of Nagas border the causeway leading to the main entrance of the Angkor Wat temple complex in Cambodia. The ancient Khmer kings of Cambodia who built the complex claimed to be descended from the union of a banished Hindu prince and a "serpent-woman," the daughter of Nagaraja, the serpent king of the land.

Buddhist Nagas

In Buddhism, Nagas are famed protectors of the Buddha and his teachings. As he sought enlightenment by meditating under the Bodhi tree, the Buddha was lashed by a storm. To shield him, the Naga Mucalinda spread his seven heads above the Buddha like a canopy, an image that is depicted in many statues. Followers of Mahayana Buddhism also believe that essential esoteric teachings were hidden by the Buddha in the underwater palaces of the Nagas, who delivered them to the brilliant Indian philosopher Nagarjuna hundreds of years after the Buddha's death.

In Tibet, Nagas are thought to dwell in lakes and underground streams, where they guard magical gems and precious stones. They also protect the purity of the water and the natural environment and retaliate against those who disturb it.

Stone sculpture of coiled Naga, 7th–8th century CE.

Niddhogg

In Norse cosmology, the Earth is imagined as a circular land surrounded by ocean. At the center of the land is a mighty ash tree called Yggdrasil whose roots go into the Underworld and whose boughs are in Heaven. The Niddhogg is a giant serpent with Dragon-like scales and claws that gnaws at the roots of the tree in the hope that the Universe will fall. It sustains itself by devouring corpses.

Other animals also live in the cosmic tree. An eagle dwells at the top, a hart feeds on the branches from whose horns mighty rivers flow, a goat gives mead for Odin's warriors rather than milk, and a nimble squirrel, Ratatosk, runs up and down the tree trunk carrying messages between Nidhogg and the eagle. Fortunately for the Universe, three wise beings called Norns repair the damage done each day by the Niddhogg by nourishing the tree's roots with water from a sacred well.

Ouroboros

In cultures the world over, the Ouroboros, a serpent curled into a circular shape so that it looks as if it is devouring its own tail, symbolizes the cycle of death and rebirth, eternity and renewal.

The Ouroboros first appeared in Egypt around 1600 BCE as an image of the circular journey of the Sun, which enters the Underworld at night and reappears each morning. In the 5th century BCE, Plato described a self-eating circular being as the first living thing—an image of self-sufficiency and perfection. An alchemy text from Alexandria, Egypt in the 2nd century CE shows a tail-eating serpent surrounding the words "All is One," a symbol of the unification of opposites.

In Norse cosmology, the Ouroboros is linked to Jörmungandr, the world-encircling serpent (see pages 58–59). On Aztec temples, it appears as a symbol of the feathered serpent Quetzalcoatl (see pages 390–391) who created the calendar. Recently, psychologists such as Carl Jung have seen the Ouroboros as a symbol of the integration of all parts of the Self, including the shadowy aspects that we reject, a process necessary for psychological wholeness.

Ouroboros

Hybrid creatures

THE HYBRID CREATURES IN THIS SECTION ENCOMPASS EVERY POSSIBLE MIXTURE OF PARTS. THEIR HEADS, TORSOS, FRONT AND HIND LEGS, TAILS, WINGS, CLAWS, AND FEET JOIN AND REJOIN IN A SEEMINGLY ENDLESS VARIETY OF IMPROBABLE COMBINATIONS.

Chimera

The Chimera is a mythical beast from Greek mythology, born from the union of Typhon and Echidna. A hybrid, it is composed of the parts of several animals. According to Homer, it is a lion in front, a snake behind, and a goat in the middle. Hesiod adds that the creature has three heads, that it is swift-footed and strong, that the beast's hindquarters are those of a Dragon and that the goat head breathes blazing fire. The creature lives in Lycia (now southern Turkey), a landscape where volcanic gas vents are common.

A classical Chimera

The tale of the vanquishing of the Chimera is told in Homer's *Iliad*. Bellerophon, the son of the king of Corinth, is forced to flee his father's city because he has committed a murder. The exiled youth arrives at Tiryns, the stronghold of King Proteus. The wife of the king takes a fancy to the youth and when he rejects her advances, she accuses him of trying to ravish her. Unwilling to kill a guest, Proteus sends Bellerophon to the court of his father-in law, King Iobates of Lycia, with sealed instructions to have him killed. To fulfill this request, Iobates gives Bellerophon an impossible task—kill the Chimera.

Told by a seer that he will need the help of the winged horse Pegasus (see pages 122–123) to accomplish this feat, Bellerophon prays to Athena, who brings him the steed. As he flies over the Chimera's head and feels the heat of its breath, Bellerophon gets an idea. He attaches a block of lead to his spear, flies head-on toward the beast and shoves the lead into its throat. The Chimera's fiery breath melts the lead, and the monster suffocates.

In medieval bestiaries, the Chimera is described as an embodiment of the deceptive or evil forces of nature. In the 14th century, a version of the beast appears in Dante's description of Hell in the *Inferno*.

Chimera

Camelopard

Ancient travelers to Egypt, India, Ethiopia, and Arabia returned to their own countries with tales of actual animals so marvelous they seemed to be mythic. Because no one in Europe had ever seen these creatures, travelers described them as being composed of parts of animals that were more familiar.

One of the best-known hybrid animals of ancient times is the Camelopard. Some believed that the spotted, long-necked creature was born from the union of a camel and a leopard. Early travelers' tales describe it as brown with white spots, with the neck of a horse, feet and legs of an ox, and the head of a camel. Today, we know the Camelopard as a giraffe. But the English word "Camelopard," which first appeared in the 14th century, remained in use until the 19th century, and the scientific name of the animal is still *Giraffa camelopardis*. The Arabic word for the creature, *ziraafa*, means "assemblage of animals."

Barometz

As with strange animals, ancient travelers explained unusual plants in terms of what they knew. Cotton, which was being cultivated and woven into cloth in Central Asia and the Middle East as early as 3000 BCE, was unknown to people in other parts of the world. A plant from whose puffy fibers cloth could be woven, medieval travelers reasoned, must be a kind of wool-producing lamb.

The Barometz, also called the Vegetable Lamb of Tartary, was believed to grow little gourds as its fruit. When the gourds were cut in two, within each was a tiny lamb. *Barometz* is the Tartar word for "lamb." Connected to the plant stalk by umbilical cords, the lambs grazed the land around the plant. When their food supply was exhausted, the lambs ran off and the plant died, or in some versions, humans and wolves ate the meat, which was said to taste like crab!

Barometz

Cynocephalus

Cynocephali

The Cynocephali—the word means "dog-heads" in Greek—were a mythical race of hybrid creatures with human bodies and dogs' heads. As described by ancient Greek writers as early as the 5th century BCE, the creatures were black and hairy, with huge necks like horses. Herodotus said that they breathed fire, barked, and lived in Ethiopia. Marco Polo claimed that they lived on an island in the Indian Ocean. Other reports placed them in India.

An Eastern Christian Orthodox tradition holds that no less a personage than St. Christopher was a Cynocephalus, as is shown in icons depicting the saint with a dog's head. Perhaps the reason behind this tradition is that Christopher came from an exotic North African Berber tribe called the Marmaritae. He was reported to be of enormous size and with a terrifying demeanor. Captured in combat by the Romans around 300 CE, he accepted baptism and began to preach the gospel. No doubt his unusual appearance converted many people.

Tikbalang

The Tikbalang is a creature from the folklore of the Philippines. The creature stands upright like a tall and powerful man, though it has the head and hooves of a horse. The forelegs, which look like arms ending with bony fingers, are long enough to touch the ground.

Tikbalangs are known to scare travelers and lead them astray. It can also imitate the voice and mannerisms of a person known to the traveler and use this ruse to lure victims into the forest from which they never return. Folk remedies to protect travelers from the Tikbalang include wearing one's shirt inside out and either calling out a warning or walking silently through the forest so as not to disturb the creature. A Tikbalang can also be tamed, but to do so a person must ride it to exhaustion and pluck one of the three thickest spines of its mane to use as a magical talisman.

Gulon

The Gulon is a creature from Scandinavian folklore described by Olaus Magnus in his *History of the Northern People* (1555). Magnus says that the creature is as large as a great dog, with the ears and face of a cat, long brown fur, a short tail, and sharp claws.

It lives in the northern snowfields and exists on carrion—the carcasses of animals killed by other predators. In northern Sweden, the creature is called a Jerff. The notoriety of the beast is due to its strange eating habits. After finding a carcass, it devours so much meat that its stomach is stretched tight like a drum. Then it finds two trees growing close together and squeezes its swollen body between them to aid digestion. That done, it returns to the carcass to eat some more! This behavior led to frequent mentions of the Gulon in bestiaries as a symbol of gluttony.

Buraq

The Buraq is the mysterious mount that carried Muhammad on a miraculous journey that is traditionally said to have been accomplished in a single night. The Buraq is described as white and long, larger than a donkey and smaller than a mule. It has the face of a woman, the wings of an eagle, and the tail feathers of a peacock. In a single stride, it is able to gallop a distance equal to the range of its vision. In Arabic, *al-buraaq* means "lightning."

Some time in 620 CE, Muhammad told his followers about the journey that he took accompanied by the Angel Gabriel. On the first part, called the Isra, Muhammad rode Buraq from Mecca to "the furthest mosque," usually identified as the Al-Aqsa Mosque in Jerusalem. On the second part, called the Miraj, the Buraq carried Muhammad from Jerusalem to Heaven and Hell, where he spoke with earlier prophets such as Abraham, Moses, and Jesus.

Buraq

Nue

Nue

The Nue is a legendary creature from Japanese folklore, sometimes called the Japanese Chimera. A hybrid of several animals, the beast has the head of a monkey, the body of a *tanuki* (raccoon dog), the legs of a tiger, and the tail of a snake. Because of its ability to transform into a black cloud and fly around, the Nue is reputed to bring misfortune and illness.

The most famous story involving a Nue is told in *The Tale of the Heike*, a classic of medieval Japanese literature. In 1153, the Emperor Konoe of Japan began to have nightmares and to fall ill. The source of his illness was a dark cloud that appeared on the palace roof each night. One night, the samurai Yorimasu Minamoto stood watch on the roof and, when the cloud appeared, shot an arrow into it. Out fell a dead Nue, which the samurai submerged in the Sea of Japan.

Manticore

The Manticore is a hybrid beast of Persian origin—in Farsi *mardkhora* means "man-slayer." According to Pliny, the creature comes from Ethiopia and has the body of a blood-red lion, the face and ears of a man, a ferocious mouth with a triple row of teeth, azure eyes, and a tail that is fanned at the end with poisonous spines.

The Manticore's call sounds like a trumpet and flute played together. A swift hunter, the creature kills its prey by shooting quills from its tail; unfortunately, its favorite food is human flesh. During the Middle Ages, the Manticore was a favorite in bestiaries and sometimes appeared as a decoration in medieval churches as an emblem of the doom-predicting Hebrew prophet Jeremiah. Today, it is said by some to roam the jungles of Indonesia, to kill its prey instantly with a bite or a scratch and to eat its victims entirely, bones and all.

Perytion

This hybrid has been described as having the head and feet of a stag and the wings of a bird. Remarkably, the shadow cast by this creature is that of a human being, which leads to the conjecture that it might be the spirit of a traveler who died far from home.

The source for this description of the Perytion comes from Argentine writer Jorge Luis Borges (1899–1986) in his marvelous 20th-century bestiary, *The Book of Imaginary Beings*. Borges quotes from a lost manuscript written by a 16th-century rabbi from Fez, who refers to the work of an Arabic author that was lost in the burning of the library at Alexandria.

Whether the Perytion existed as a mythical creature in antiquity cannot be proved, though Borges tells the story of an attack by a band of Perytions on the Roman commander Scipio and his army during their invasion of Carthage. Since each Perytion can kill only one man, much of the army survived, and the Roman campaign succeeded.

Yale

The Yale, also called a Centicore, is a hybrid creature from European legends about the size of a goat. The name may derive from the Hebrew word *ya-el*, which means "mountain goat."

The parts of other animals of which the beast is composed vary with the source. According to Pliny, the Yale is black or tawny in color, with the tail of an elephant, and the jaws of a boar. The beast's most remarkable feature is its long straight horns, which can be pointed forward or sloped backward according to whether they are needed for defense. Some medieval bestiaries gave the creature multicolored spots, the head of a goat and the feet of a Unicorn.

Because of its swiveling horns, the Yale was adapted into heraldry with the meaning of "proud defense." Yale supporters appear on the coat of arms of England's Beaufort family and can be seen over the gateway of Christ's College, Cambridge.

Yale

Satyr

Satyr

Satyrs are the rural fertility spirits of ancient Greece. From the waist down, they are lusty goats, above, they are men, though their arms and upper bodies are covered with hair. Their faces have upturned animal noses and pointy ears, with goat horns on their foreheads and wreaths of ivy curling through their hair.

As companions of the god of wine Dionysus, their pastimes are drinking, dancing, playing tambourines and flutes, and sporting with Nymphs. Men dressed as Satyrs served as the chorus in plays performed at ancient Greek festivals to Dionysus.

Though a devotee of Artemis and vowed to chastity, the Nymph Syrinx was pursued by a lusty Satyr in a story told in Ovid's *Metamorphoses*. Her desperate prayers answered, Syrinx was transformed into hollow water reeds by sympathetic river Nymphs and so escaped her amorous pursuer. Frustrated, the Satyr fashioned the reeds into a set of panpipes on which he blew a haunting melody.

Crocotta and Leucrotta

The offspring of mythical beasts are sometimes more outrageous than their parents, as with the monstrous children of Echidna and Typhon. According to Pliny, the Leucrotta is the offspring of a Crocotta and a lion, though aside from powerful jaws, the creatures have little in common.

The Crocotta is a combination of wolf and dog, with impossibly strong teeth and the uncanny ability to lure by imitating the human voice both dogs and men into the forest in order to devour them. Its offspring, the Leucrotta, is about the size of the wild ass, with the legs of a stag, the neck, tail, and breast of a lion, the head of a badger, cloven hooves, and an enormous mouth that extends up to its ears. Instead of teeth, it has a horizontal blade of bone between the upper and lower jaws. Like the Crocotta, the beast's voice imitates a human laugh, which hints that its description fits the hyena.

Baku

Baku

This helpful hybrid creature from Japanese folklore looks something like an enormous tapir or a wild pig. Folk descriptions say that it has the compact body of a horse, the face of a lion, the trunk and tusks of an elephant, the tail of a cow, and the feet of a tiger.

The Baku repels wickedness. In China, where the creature originated, it was believed that sleeping on a Baku pelt could protect a person from pestilence and that its image was a powerful talisman against evil. In Japan, the Baku is famed as the "eater of dreams," said to be caused by evil spirits. A person awakening from a nightmare should call three times saying, "Baku, eat my dreams." Thus summoned, the Baku will turn bad omens into good fortune by devouring evil influences. The *kanji* character for its name used to be painted on pillows as a protection for sleepers.

Ahuizotl

The Ahuizotl is a mythological creature from the folklore of Aztec Mexico. Its name means "water monster" in Náhuatl, the Aztec language. About the size of a small dog, the creature is smooth, slippery, and black, with a simian face and a monkey's prehensile fingers. At the tip of its tail is a human-shaped hand.

The bane of fishermen, the Ahuizotl lures its victims to the water's edge by imitating a fish and then grabs the person with the hand at the end of its tail to pull him or her into the depths. Three days later, the victim's body floats to the surface, unblemished but missing its eyes, teeth, and nails, delicacies on which the Ahuizotl loves to feast. According to the *Florentine Codex*, a manuscript of Aztec lore written in Náhuatl and Spanish in the 16th century, when the Ahuizotl was unable to catch and drown a victim, it had been heard to cry like a baby.

Legendary creatures

THESE CREATURES ARE LARGER, MORE FEROCIOUS, MORE TERRIFYING,
OR MORE WONDERFUL THAN ORDINARY ANIMALS. THE QUARRY OF THE
HEROES OF LEGEND, SOME HAVE MAGICAL ABILITIES; OTHERS ARE SO
FRIGHTENING THAT THEY CAUSE PEOPLE TO PANIC, EVEN TODAY.

Cu Sith

Cu Sith (pronounced "coo shee") is the legendary fairy hound of the Scottish Highlands. An enormous canine about the size of a large calf, Cu Sith is dark green in color, with shaggy fur and a long braided or curled tail.

It makes its lair in clefts in the rocks. The beast's immense footprints have been found in the mud, in the snow, and on the sand. At Luskentyre on the Scottish Isle of Harris, the fairy hound has been known to leave paw prints on the damp sand that suddenly vanish halfway across the beach.

Though it often hunts silently on the fog-shrouded moors, the Cu Sith has a loud and terrifying bark that can be heard over long distances, even by ships at sea. When the hound barks three times, women are careful to lock their doors, as the beast has been known to abduct nursing mothers to supply milk for fairy babies.

Fenris

Fenris is an enormous evil wolf in Norse mythology. Though shaped like a wolf, the beast is so enormous that when he opens his mouth, his upper jaw touches the heavens.

Because of a prophecy that Fenris and his offspring will be responsible for the destruction of the Earth, the gods keep him locked in a cage and bound with a magical chain called Gleipnir fashioned by the Dwarves. Gleipnir is composed of six strange things: the footsteps of a cat, the roots of a mountain, a woman's beard, the breath of fishes, the sinews of a bear, and a

The god Tyr sacrifices his hand in order to bind the Fenris Wolf.

bird's spittle. No matter how hard Fenris struggles, he is unable break this chain. In revenge, he bites off the hand of Tyr, the Norse war god, who is the only one brave enough to feed him. At Ragnarök, the end of the world, Fenris will break his chain and join the Giants in their battle against the gods.

American folklore creatures

Among the legendary creatures of American folklore, three that have enjoyed particular fame are the Wampus cat, the Jersey Devil, and the Jackalope.

Wampus Cat

The Wampus Cat, a huge feline, half-mountain lion and half-woman, stalks the forests of eastern Tennessee. According to Cherokee legend, the Wampus Cat used to be a beautiful Native American woman. One night, the woman hid behind a rock under the hide of a mountain cat to listen to the sacred stories told by men around the campfire. When she was discovered, a medicine man punished her for eavesdropping on the lore by transforming her into a monstrous cat. Now she roams the hills and forests howling to protest her fate and seeking revenge.

Jersey Devil

The Jersey Devil is a two-legged flying creature, with a horse's head and the long neck, wings, and tail of a devil. It lives in the Pine Barrens, a forested region along the coast of southern New Jersey. The creature was born in the 18th century as the 13th child of Deborah Smith Leeds who had settled in the Pine Barrens. Because she cursed her unborn child, it was born with cloven hooves, claws, and a tail. During a week of terror in January 1909, thousands of people claimed to have seen the creature, causing mass hysteria across the state.

Jackalope

The Jackalope of Wyoming is said to be a cross between the pygmy-deer and a killer rabbit. Stuffed specimens are displayed in many towns in the American West. According to legend, Jackalope milk has medicinal uses, the Jackalope can imitate the human voice and does so to lead pursuers astray, and the rarity of Jackalopes can be explained by their inability to breed except during electrical storms that include hail. Interestingly, during the 16th to 18th centuries, some European naturalists believed in the existence of horned rabbits and pictured them in books of curiosities.

Jackalope

Griffin and Hippogriff

One of the best-known legendary animals is the Griffin, a combination of eagle and lion that has been known in Mesopotamia and Egypt since 3300 BCE. From the Griffin we derive the Hippogriff, the result of a union between a Griffin and a mare.

Griffin

Most often, the beast has the body of a lion and the head, wings, legs, and talons of an eagle. Said to be the offspring of the king of beasts and the king of birds, the Griffin was considered to be particularly powerful and majestic.

A legend says that Alexander the Great (356—323 BCE) harnessed eight Griffins to a basket in which he flew into the heavens.

Griffin

Like dragons, Griffins were said to guard treasure and to be especially fierce in defending their hoard. Often pictured in bestiaries, Griffins were emblems of regal courage, as they were when they appeared on coats of arms. In medieval Christianity, the Griffin's combination of an earthly beast and a bird of the air led to its use as a symbol for Christ's human and divine qualities combined. For this reason, Griffins were often sculpted on churches.

Hippogriffs

Because horses were said to be the favourite prey of Griffins, when the two species did mate, their offspring were rare and fabulous. As conceived in medieval European folklore, the Hippogriff was part-horse and part-Griffin. Like a Griffin, the creature has the head and beak of an eagle, claws with talons and wings covered with feathers, but the rest of its body is a horse.

The Hippogriff was a favorite creature in medieval poems and fables. A Hippogriff is featured in the epic poem *Orlando Furioso* (1516) by Italian author Ludovico Ariosto. Because the creature makes an excellent steed that flies as fast as lightning, it serves as the mount of the wizard Atlante and carries the poem's heroes on quests to rescue various maidens. Today, the creature is enjoying new interest because of the role of the Hippogriff Buckbeak in the Harry Potter series.

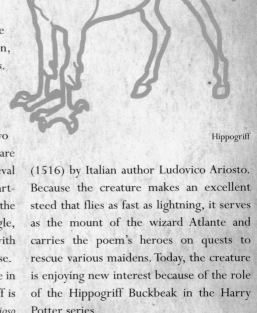

Hippogriff

Questing Beast and White Hart

The legends surrounding King Arthur include the stories of a number of mythical creatures, some foreboding and some wonderfully mystical, including the Questing Beast and the White Hart.

Questing Beast

The Questing Beast is a strange hybrid with the head and neck of a serpent, the body of a leopard, the hindquarters of a lion, and the feet of a stag. Its name comes not from the fact that it is quested after, but from the sound it makes, described as the barking of 20 pairs of hounds on the quest.

In Sir Thomas Malory's *Le Morte d'Arthur* (1485), the Questing Beast appears to Arthur after he has unknowingly slept with his half-sister Morgause; it is their son Mordred who eventually brings about Arthur's death (see page 261). Hot on the trail of the Questing Beast is Sir Pellinore, who tells Arthur that he has been tracking the beast his entire life. Merlin reveals that the Questing Beast is the offspring of an incestuous union between a royal brother and sister. Though Arthur is not yet aware that he, too, has been party to incest, the reader understands the Questing Beast as a prophecy of the final doom of Arthur's kingdom.

White Hart

Another beast sought by Arthurian knights is the White Hart. At the wedding feast of Arthur and Guinevere, a magical White Hart rides into the hall and circles the Round Table, pursued by 60 black hounds and one smaller white one. When one of Arthur's knights makes off with the white hound, a lady on horseback rides in protesting that the white hound is hers. When an armed knight carries the lady away, Merlin explains that these magical events are not to be taken lightly. They signal the beginning of marvelous adventures, both knightly and amorous, as the appearance of a White Hart always does in medieval legends. The pun on "hart" and "heart," as in a knight "killing his lady's hart," occurs frequently in courtly romances.

White Hart

Pegasus

Pegasus is a flying horse in Greek mythology, usually pictured as a majestic white stallion with powerful wings. The story most often told about his birth is that the steed sprang from the neck of the snake-haired goddess Medusa when she was beheaded by the hero Perseus (see pages 232–233). After his birth, Pegasus flew to Mount Helicon, the home of the Muses, the Nymphs who inspire creative expression. When he stamped the ground with his hoof, a freshwater spring arose. Called the Hippocrene or "Horse Spring," its water was believed to be a source of poetic inspiration.

You have already heard the story of Bellerophon, the hero who was riding Pegasus when he slew the Chimera (see pages 98–99). Bellerophon was so proud of this feat that he tried to ride to the top of Mount Olympus to join the gods. But Pegasus threw the presumptuous hero off his back. When he died, Pegasus achieved immortality as a starry constellation.

Sleipnir

Sleipnir is the eight-legged horse of Odin, the chief god in Norse mythology. Swift and fearless, with a giant stride, the beast carried Odin in the eight directions of the heavens.

This creature came into being when a rock giant, disguised as a stone mason, was contracted to repair the wall around Asgard, the home of the gods, within six months. In return, the gods promised him the goddess Freya as well as the Sun and the Moon. With the help of his stallion Svalidfari, the mason made such rapid progress that the gods were worried they would have to pay up. So the trickster god Loki transformed himself into a mare and lured Svalidfari away. Angry that the wall could not be completed in time, the mason revealed his true form, and the god Thor killed him with a hammer blow. Months later, Loki presented Odin with the offspring of his union with Svalidfari—the magical eight-legged colt Sleipnir.

Pegasus

Centaur

The Centaurs are a legendary race of creatures—part-man and part-horse—in Greek mythology and are generally depicted as having the body and legs of a horse joined to the torso and head of a man.

Most Greek writers considered the Centaurs to be uncivilized, lusty, quick to fight, and easily intoxicated. At the wedding of Pirithous, the king of Lapith, a band of Centaurs got drunk and tried to carry off the bride and the female guests. In the battle that ensued, many Centaurs were killed.

Centaur

Origins

Several stories are told about the origin of the Centaurs. According to some Greek writers, the Centaurs are the sons of Ixion, the father of Pirithous and the cloud Nymph Nephele, who at the time had assumed the shape of Hera, queen of the gods. Others say that the creatures were the offspring of Centaurus, a son of the god Apollo and the mares of Magnesium. Still others say that Zeus himself fathered the Centaurs when he transformed himself into a stallion and lay with Dia, the wife of Ixion.

Though a few Centaurs have been notable for their nobility, civilized Centaurs were an exception. When Pholus, a noble Centaur, was entertaining the Greek hero Hercules, he could not refuse his guest's request for wine. But as soon as the jar was uncorked, other Centaurs nearby were driven mad by the scent and attacked Hercules, who drove them off with poisoned arrows (see page 329).

Chiron and Achilles

Chiron

The noblest Centaur was Chiron, revered for his knowledge and skill in medicine. He tutored many Greek heroes: including Achilles, the pre-eminent Greek warrior of the Trojan War; Jason, who captained the Argonauts on the quest for the Golden Fleece; and Aesclepius, the most famous physician of the Greek world. Chiron taught his young apprentice the art of surgery and the use of drugs, incantations, and potions.

Water creatures

SOME WATER CREATURES ARE KNOWN TO BE UNPREDICTABLE AND
DANGEROUS IN THEIR DEALINGS WITH HUMANKIND. THESE INCLUDE
MERMAIDS AND OTHER MERFOLK, THE UNSEEN INHABITANTS OF THE
WORLD'S WATERS, WHO MAGICALLY SHAPE-SHIFT AND LIVE ON LAND.
THEY ARE SUPERNATURALLY LOVELY OR FIERCELY TERRIFYING. OTHER
CREATURES, SUCH AS NEREIDS AND NAIADS, ARE KNOWN TO HARBOR
KINDLY FEELINGS TOWARD HUMANS AND OFFER PROTECTION AND
HEALING TO THOSE THEY ENCOUNTER.

Mermaids

Mermaids are legendary water creatures
that have appeared in the mythology of
peoples around the world from earliest
times. Though mermen also figure in these
stories, in most cultures, the Mermaid is a
powerful feminine presence.

Aspects of the Goddess

In ancient cultures ringing the
Mediterranean, Mermaids were regarded as
semi-divine aspects of the Goddess,
connected to the sea from which life arises
and honored in seaside temples. The earliest
Mermaid story comes from Assyria around
1000 BCE. Atargatis, an Assyrian priestess,
jumped into the sea to wash away the shame
of an unwanted pregnancy and emerged as
a fishtailed goddess. In the 2nd century
BCE, the Greek historian Lucian reported
that the statue of the Great Goddess at the
temple of Hieropolis (now modern Turkey)
had a fishtail instead of legs. In Greece,
Aphrodite, the goddess of love, was born
from the sea foam and rode to land on a
half-scallop shell.

In the 1st century CE, Pliny wrote
convincingly of the existence of Mermaids,
but said that their bodies were "rough and
scaled all over." But by the 5th century CE,

In Japan the story is told of a fisherman who catches a Ningyo, grills it and serves it to his guests. Afraid to eat the fish because of its human face, one of the guests wraps his portion in paper to take home and discard. But the man's young daughter eats ʿhe fish while her father is drunk on sake. At in st the father is worried, but the girl ʾers no ill effects—except that after she rom arried, she remains youthful, even as come sband ages and dies. After marrying shed t ing widowed many times, the still- the roc l woman becomes a Buddhist nun, Selkies anders and teaches for 800 years becom her life ends.

have c

stories *kyawk*

Selkie ous Australian people honor a realskin spirit that lives in sacred water-Nhe sea lled a Yawkyawk, these spirits often Iesolate. Mermaids, young women with Nnely fishe long green hair like seaweed or cu to the sea s of seaweed or green algae Naerge fr ha her. pro

ι

dang

floating in the water are said to be Yawkyawk hair.

Like the Greek Naiads, Yawkyawks are fertility spirits. Just going near a waterhole where a Yawkyawk lives can make a woman pregnant. Linked to life-giving water, Yawkyawks bring the rains that provide drinking water and make the plants grow, but if they are angry, that can bring violent storms. Yawkyawks are shape-shifters and can sometimes take the form of a crocodile, a swordfish, or a snake. Sometimes Yawkyawks grow legs and walk the land at night. Other times, they grow wings and fly about like dragonflies. Like Mermaids, Yawkyawks sometimes marry human men, but the marriages end when the Yawkyawks return to the water.

Some Indigenous Australian peoples say that the Yawkyawk is the daughter of the creator spirit Ngalyod, the Rainbow Serpent (see page 67). Others say that the two are aspects of the same divine being.

Mami Wata and Jengu

Mami Wata and Jengu are female water spirits honored in Africa, the Caribbean, and parts of North and South America.

Mami Wata

In the oldest versions of her mythology, Mami Wata is a Mermaid with the upper body of a woman and the lower body of a fish or reptile. When she appears as a human woman, she is elegant and exceptionally beautiful, with brilliant eyes, a lighter than normal complexion, attractive clothes in the latest fashion, an abundance of shiny jewelry, and excessively long hair that she is fond of brushing back with a golden comb. In both her Mermaid and human forms, Mami Wata carries expensive baubles, such as watches, combs, and mirrors. She is frequently accompanied by a large snake, a symbol of psychic power and divinity in many African cultures.

Like other mermaids, Mami Wata is unpredictable in her interactions with humans. Legends say that she may kidnap swimmers and take them to her underwater realm, releasing them when they promise fidelity to her cult. This legend may be related to the belief that she is responsible for the strong undertow that kills many swimmers along the coast. However, she is also believed to gift her followers with material wealth and spiritual accomplishments. At shrines in her honor, devotees wearing red and white, Mami Wata's sacred colors, dance until they have been possessed by her spirit, and receive her advice and blessings.

Jengu

A water spirit similar to Mami Wata is honored in Cameroon. Called a Jengu (plural Miengu), this beautiful Mermaid-like creature has long, woolly hair and a gap-toothed smile. Miengu are said to inhabit rivers and the sea. Believed to be beneficent, they carry messages between the people who honor them and the world of spirits. They also cure illnesses and bless their devotees with good luck, protection from epidemics, victory in competitions, and fair weather.

is often pic...
chariot drawn
often ride on then
in Rome has winge
Neptune's (Poseidon's) ...

In Greek legend, whe...
Argonauts were unsure of the...
quest for the Golden Fleece, the...
in amazement as a giant Hippocan...
unhitched from Poseidon's chariot, ...
rose from the sea and galloped away acro...

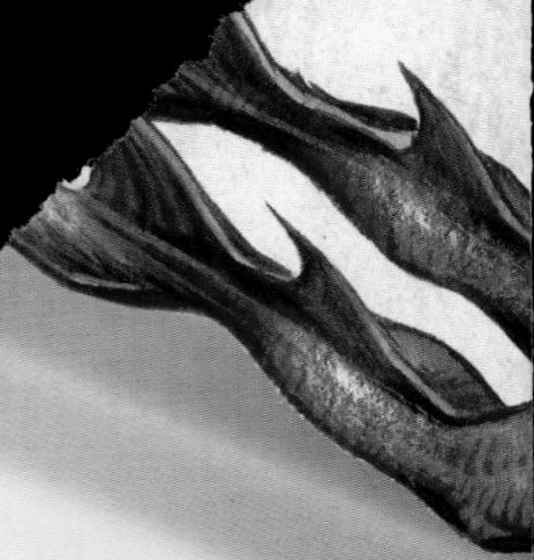

us

, but

rse-like

aggy coat.   encounters—in 1890,
e in rivers, lakes,   Melbourne Zoo tried and
gs (parts of rivers that failed to capture a Bunyip that had
course of the river has   been seen repeatedly near Victoria.
nyips defend their lairs by Bunyips are a favorite creature for
blood-curdling cries and by cryptozoologists who theorize that the
evouring intruders. Bunyip mothers can beast may be a descendant of a prehistoric
also cause devastating floods if humans marsupial. To Indigenous Australians,
disturb their offspring. When a Bunyip's cry however, the Bunyip is a spirit of the
is heard, Indigenous Australians avoid Dreamtime—the oral tradition that tells
water sources. During the 19th century, the stories of the origins of the land and
Australian settlers reported many Bunyip its people.

Adaro

Adaro

The Adaro are malevolent Mermen-like sea spirits in the mythology of the Solomon Islands. Believed to embody the wicked part of a dead man's spirit, the creatures are human in shape, with gills behind the ears, fins instead of feet, a shark-like dorsal fin, and a swordfish-like spear growing out of the head.

Adaros are said to live in the Sun and to travel back and forth to Earth by sliding along rainbows. They also travel via sun showers and waterspouts. Adaros are dangerous to humans and kill by shooting people in the neck with poisonous flying fish. Their chief is named Ngorieru and is said to live off the coast of San Christobal. Canoes passing his haunt dip their paddles quietly, and people speak in low voices so as not to attract his attention. However, Adaros also visit men in their dreams to teach them new songs and dances.

Kappa

A Kappa is a water sprite from Japanese folklore. The size of a small child—the word *kappa* means "river child" in Japanese —the creature has green, scaly skin, a body like a frog or a tortoise, webbed fingers and toes, and a monkey or duck-like head and face.

The source of a Kappa's power is a fluid-filled depression at the top of its skull. If the liquid spills from this cavity, the Kappa is weakened and may die. To outwit a Kappa, make a deep bow, which the Kappa will return, causing the liquid to spill.

According to legend, Kappas catch and eat children who are swimming in rivers and ponds. To protect them, parents write their children's names on cucumbers and throw them into the pond as gifts for the Kappas, since cucumbers are the only food Kappas like more than children! The name "Kappa Maki" for cucumber-filled sushi rolls derives from this folk belief.

Grindylow

A Grindylow is a pale green water demon that lives in the weed beds at the bottom of lakes in Britain. In the folklore of Yorkshire, the creature is described as humanoid in shape, with long arms, long, brittle fingers, sharp little horns, and small green teeth.

Like the Japanese Kappa, the Grindylow is said to use its long arms to grab small children who venture too near the edge of ponds and marshes, pull them into the water, and eat them. Recently, Grindylows appeared in contemporary literature as the mythical creatures in the lake near Hogwarts in *Harry Potter and the Goblet of Fire*.

In other English counties, similar water demons are envisioned as hags, with green skin, long seaweed-like hair, and sharp teeth. Called Peg Powler near the River Tees in northern England and Jinny Greenteeth in Lancashire, the legendary creatures may have arisen as a way of frightening young children away from dangerous pools of water.

Grindylow

140

Bishop Fish

Bishop Fish

One of the most unusual sea creatures in medieval European folklore was the Bishop Fish, also called the "Sea Monk" or "Sea Bishop." It looks like a giant fish, but its tail fins resemble legs wearing fisherman's boots and its pectoral fins are claw-like fingers. The creature's head is cone-shaped like a bishop's miter (conical hat). The creature was pictured in a work by Swiss naturalist Konrad von Gesner entitled *Historia Animalium* (1551–1558).

According to legend, a Bishop Fish was captured off the coast of Poland or Germany in 1531. When it was shown to a group of bishops, the creature gestured with its claw-like hands, asking to be released. The bishops agreed, the creature made the sign of the cross and disappeared into the sea. In the early 1850s, Danish zoologist Japetus Steenstrup theorized that the captured Bishop Fish may have been a giant squid and published drawings illustrating the comparison. Others have speculated the creature was really an angel shark, walrus, or hooded seal.

Cetus

Cetus is a huge sea monster that has been known since antiquity. It is closely related to Leviathan, the sea monster mentioned in the Bible, and to Tiamat, the sea monster killed by the Babylonian hero Marduk (see pages 282–283). It has the head of a dog or a dragon, the bloated body of a whale or a dolphin, and large fan-shaped fins. Hebrew and Arab astronomers identified the creature with a large constellation in the southern sky shaped like a whale.

In Greek mythology, Cetus was a sea monster sent by Poseidon to destroy a Phoenician kingdom whose queen, Cassiopeia, had boasted that she was more beautiful than Hera, queen of the gods and wife of Poseidon's brother Zeus. An oracle decreed that the only way to appease the monster was to sacrifice Cassiopeia's daughter Andromeda. So the girl was chained to a rock on the shore to be fed to the creature. But Perseus, flying home on Pegasus after killing Medusa, rescued Andromeda and married her.

Kraken

The Kraken is a giant sea creature in the legends of Norway and northern Scandinavia. A colossal octopus or squid-like creature the size of a small island, Kraken are said to be able to encircle a ship with their arms and drag the vessel under the waves. Equally dangerous is the powerful whirlpool created when the creature submerges that can suck down any ship that escapes its grasp.

During the 17th and 18th centuries, Kraken existed on the border between mythical creatures and real animals. Sailors' yarns fueled Kraken legends, and the poem "The Kraken" by Alfred Lord Tennyson (1830) linked the creature to the mythical Leviathan that will rise from the depths at the end of days. Yet, claims that an attack by Krakens was responsible for the disappearance of ten British warships in 1782 proved to be erroneous. In 1857, the Kraken moved from myth to reality with proof of the existence of the giant squid.

Kraken

Boto

Encantato

Encantato means "enchanted one" in Brazilian Portuguese. In South American folklore, the term refers to creatures from an underwater paradise called Encante. The most common Encantato is the Boto, a large and primitive-looking Amazon River dolphin that has the ability to turn into a human being.

Many traditional stories tell of a Boto that becomes a handsome young man who seduces a girl, impregnates her, then returns to the river and reverts to his dolphin form. Encantatos are also believed to abduct humans with whom they fall in love or the children born from their human love affairs, to take them to their underwater realm. Encantatos love music and parties and often transform themselves into humans to attend fiestas. When in human form, the creatures wear a hat to hide their prominent dolphin-shaped forehead. Encantatos are also believed to be able to control storms and to "enchant" human beings into doing what they command.

Salmon of Wisdom

To the ancient Celts, the salmon had mysterious powers, which were visible each year when the fish returned to their birthplace to mate and spawn. In this cycle, Irish bards saw a parallel to their own practice of repeating the traditional cycles of oral tales in which their wisdom was encoded.

The Salmon of Wisdom (in Gaelic *bradán feasa*) appears in the Fenian Cycle of Irish mythology, a group of stories and poems that tell of the exploits of the mythical hero Fionn mac Cumhail.

Originally an ordinary salmon, the fish swam in the Fountain of Wisdom, out of which five rivers flowed, including the River Boyne and the River Shannon. Around the Fountain of Wisdom grew nine hazel trees that dropped nine hazelnuts into the water. When the salmon ate the hazelnuts, it gained all the knowledge in the world. The first person to eat this salmon would gain this knowledge in turn.

Catching wisdom

For seven long years, the druid poet Finn Eces fished in the River Boyne for the Salmon of Wisdom. When he finally caught the fish, he told his apprentice Fionn to cook it for him. While the Salmon was cooking, some of the hot fat spattered on Fionn's thumb. To ease the burning pain, the boy put his thumb into his mouth and so tasted the Salmon. Then Fionn brought the cooked fish to his master—as soon as he looked into the boy's eyes, Finn Eces saw what had happened.

The knowledge Fionn gained from eating the Salmon of Wisdom allowed him to become the leader of the Fianna, the famous heroes of Irish myth. Three skills in particular were the Salmon's legacy: magic, great insight, and a poet's gift for language. Perhaps people attributed magical powers to the Salmon because of the striking rainbow-like colors of its scales. Whenever they were needed, Fionn could access these gifts by putting his thumb into his mouth.

Salmon of Wisdom

Air creatures

CREATURES OF THE AIR——REAL AND IMAGINARY BIRDS——APPEAR IN
THE MYTHOLOGY OF MANY CULTURES. THE PHOENIX IS JUST SUCH A
BIRD BUT THERE ARE OTHER FABULOUS BIRDS STRONG ENOUGH TO
LIFT ELEPHANTS, VALIANT ENOUGH TO ATTACK DEMONS, OR SO
MAGICAL THAT THEY ALTER THE WEATHER, BRINGING A DELUGE
OF RAIN OR A WEEK OF FAIR SKIES IN MID-WINTER.

Phoenix

Probably the best-known mythical creature of the air, the Phoenix has its origins in ancient Egypt. The legend was developed further by Greek and Roman writers and by the compilers of medieval bestiaries.

Egyptian mythologies

Known in Egypt as the Bennu, the bird was pictured in hieroglyphic images as a long-legged gray heron with a two-feathered crest. In some, the Bennu wears the headdress of Osiris, the god who dies and is reborn. In the mythology of Heliopolis, the city of the Sun, the Bennu was the "soul" of the Sun god Ra and was linked symbolically to the rising and setting Sun, the yearly Nile floods and the cycle of birth, death and resurrection. The word *bennu* probably comes from *weben*, which means "rise" or "shine."

Greek interpretations

The Greek historian Herodotus (5th century BCE) describes the life cycle of the Egyptian Phoenix, which he likened to an eagle with red and gold plumage. Every 500 years, the bird comes to Heliopolis from Arabia bringing its father's ashes. It embalms the remains in an egg made of myrrh and deposits them in the Temple of the Sun. At the end of its life, the bird builds a nest of incense twigs, lies down in it and dies. From its dead body, a small worm

Bennu

emerges that the heat of the Sun transforms into a new Phoenix.

The bestiaries of the Middle Ages further embellished the legend. According to the *Aberdeen Bestiary*, only one Phoenix exists at a time. It lives for upward of 500 years. At the end of its life, it builds a pyre of aromatic twigs, turns to face the rays of the Sun, fans the fire by beating its wings and is consumed by the flames. From the ashes, a new Phoenix is born. Like the Egyptians, medieval Christian writers saw in this myth a symbol of Resurrection and the hope of life after death.

Feng Huang

In China, the phoenix is called Feng Huang. Next to the Dragon, the Feng Huang is the most respected mythical creature in China and reigns over all other birds. Descriptions of the Feng Huang vary, but most emphasize the bird's fiery and colorful tail feathers, which resemble those of a peacock. The bird's head and body are like a pheasant.

Symbols of yin/yang

Originally, the Feng Huang was two birds. Feng was the male or yang bird, symbol of the solar cycle, and Huang was the female or yin bird, symbol of the lunar cycle. Pictures of the male and female birds together symbolized undying love between husband and wife. For this reason, Feng Huang decorations were commonplace at weddings. Later, the male and female birds melded into one female creature, the symbol of the Chinese empress, especially when paired with the Dragon, the symbol of the Chinese emperor.

According to legend, Feng Huang first appeared to the Emperor Huang Di around 2600 BCE. Like the Chinese Unicorn Ch'i lin, the appearance of the bird signaled a time of prosperity and marked the ascension to the throne of a benevolent new emperor. This belief is reflected in the Chinese saying: 'When the Dragon soars and the Phoenix dances, the people will enjoy happiness for years, bringing peace and tranquillity to all under heaven.'

Immortal

Unlike the Western Phoenix, the Feng Huang is immortal. It embodies the five virtues of benevolence, righteousness, propriety, wisdom, and sincerity. According to Chinese mythology, it is one of the four celestial creatures that rule the quadrants of Heaven. The green Dragon rules the east and the spring; the white tiger rules the west and the summer; the black tortoise rules the north and the winter; and the red Phoenix rules the south and the autumn.

Feng Huang

Simurgh

The Simurgh is the mythical bird of Persia, so old it has seen the destruction of the Universe three times over. An immense creature the shape of a peacock with spectacular plumage, it has the claws of a lion and is large enough to carry off an elephant or a whale.

In a classic of Sufi literature entitled *The Conference of the Birds* by Farid ud-Din Attar, a thousand birds follow a feather dropped by the Simurgh. After journeying through seven valleys and overcoming a hundred difficulties and trials, 30 birds arrive at the Simurgh's dwelling place. The name Simurgh can be translated as "30 birds." When they see the Simurgh, the birds realize that there is no such thing as individual identity—they are the Simurgh and the Simurgh is them. Like drops falling into the ocean, they annihilate themselves gloriously in the Simurgh and find mystical peace, joy, and immortality.

Firebird

In Russian folklore, the Firebird is a magical bird with majestic plumage that glows red, orange, and yellow, like a bonfire. In Russian, its name is *Zhar-Ptitsa*, which means "heat bird." At midnight, the bird comes into gardens to eat the golden apples of immortality and to light up the night. When it sings, pearls fall from its beak.

The Firebird appears in a famous Russian fairy tale in which Prince Ivan, the youngest son of the tsar, finds the tail feather of the Firebird and embarks on a fabulous quest to bring the bird back to his father's kingdom. Along the way, Ivan overcomes the treachery of his two older brothers, receives help from a magical gray wolf, wins a horse with a golden mane, rescues a beautiful princess, dies, and is resurrected by the magical water of life and death, and returns to his father's house on a flying carpet carrying the Firebird in a golden cage.

Firebird

Harpies

Harpies are hideous creatures with the bodies of birds and the white faces of women who are pale with a hunger that can never be satisfied. Often called the "snatchers," they swoop down to grab the food of others with their curved claws and foul the table with their excrement.

Harpies are among the terrible offspring of Echidna and Typhon (see page 91) and appear in the sagas of two Classical heroes, Jason and Aeneas. Phineas, the king of Thrace, was being punished by Zeus for misusing his prophetic gift and revealing too much about the future. He was exiled to an island where a lavish banquet table was always set. But every time Phineas sat down to eat, the Harpies swooped down, stole the food from his hands and spoiled the rest.

This torture continued until the arrival of Jason and the Argonauts. Two of the members of the crew were sons of Boreas, the North Wind. Because they could fly, they chased away the Harpies but did not kill them at the request of their sister Iris, the rainbow goddess. Iris promised that her terrible sisters would not torment Phineas again. In gratitude, Phineas provided guidance to the Argonauts for the next part of their quest.

Harpy

Harpy

Legend of Aeneas

Aeneas, another mythical hero and Trojan warrior sailed to Italy to found the city of Rome, but lost his way in a storm. After four days, his ship docked on an island in the Ionian Sea. Exhausted and hungry, Aeneas and his crew prepared a feast from the abundant cattle on the island, but as soon as they sat down to eat, the Harpies swooped down and snatched the meal. Twice more the Harpies descended. The third time, the Trojans fought back and Celaeno, the leader of the Harpies, cursed the Trojans saying that they would not land in their promised city until they, too, had experienced terrible hunger.

Roc

The Roc, also called the *Rukh*, is an enormous, white bird of prey in Middle Eastern legend. It resembles an eagle or a vulture with a massive wingspan. Marco Polo reported having seen a Roc at the court of Kublai Khan whose talons were strong enough to carry off an elephant.

The Roc is featured in one of the adventures of Sinbad the Sailor in the collection of Persian folktales sometimes called *The Book of One Thousand and One Nights* or simply *Arabian Nights* (c.800–900 CE). After a shipwreck, Sinbad finds himself marooned on an island with nothing but brushwood and a huge spherical dome. To his horror, he discovers that the dome is an enormous egg and that he is in the nest of a giant bird. When the bird returns, he ties himself to its leg with his turban and rides high into the sky, escaping when the Roc flies near a less dangerous island.

Ba-bird

The Ba-bird is an aspect of ancient Egyptian beliefs about the afterlife. A person's Ba is his or her distinctive essence, all of the non-physical qualities that make up the personality.

Shaped like a sparrow hawk or small falcon, each Ba-bird has the face of the deceased human being of which it is part. Images painted on Egyptian tombs often show the Ba-bird hovering over the body of the deceased. Closely linked to the physical body, the Ba-bird was believed to require physical sustenance, such as food and drink.

In ancient Egyptian beliefs, in order for a deceased person to achieve immortality, the body needed to leave the tomb to unite with the person's Ka or life force. As the mummified physical body can no longer do this, the person's Ba transforms into a bird that can fly between the tomb and the Ka in the Underworld land of the dead. This journey needs to happen every night.

Roc

Painting of Vishnu and Lakshmi on Garuda, c.1700.

Garuda

The Garuda is a large bird-like creature in Hindu and Buddhist mythology. In Hindu legend, the Garuda generally has the golden body of a man, with an eagle's beak, red wings, and a white face. Often wearing a crown, the creature is ancient and huge enough to block out the Sun.

The Hindu epic the *Mahabharata* includes an account of the Garuda's birth and deeds. When he burst from the egg blazing with the fire that consumes the Universe at the end of an eon, even the gods were terrified, so the Garuda reduced his size and energy.

The gift of immortality

To win the release of his mother, the Garuda agreed to steal *amrita*, the elixir of immortality, from the gods and bring it to the Nagas (see pages 94–95). After overcoming the terrifying defenses erected by the gods, the Garuda took the elixir in his mouth and, without swallowing it, flew back to the Nagas. On the way, he met the god Vishnu who gave the Garuda the gift of immortality if the bird would agree to become his mount. The Garuda also promised the god Indra to help the gods regain the elixir after his mother had been freed. Making good on these promises, the Garuda became Vishnu's trusted mount and the relentless enemy of the Naga kingdom.

Tibetan versions

In Tibetan Buddhism, the Garuda is often depicted with a bulging belly and big eyes, short blue horns, and yellow hair standing on end. The Garuda is daring and fearless, with the strength and power to sail over obstacles. In some images, the bird is holding two snakes in its talons. In Buddhist iconography, the snake represents hatred and the Garuda symbolizes the spiritual energy that overcomes it. Soaring through space, the Garuda stands for the open freedom of mind unfettered by negative emotions such as anger and jealousy; and for the keen insight that recognizes hatred when it arises in the mind so that, like a bird of prey, we can swoop down and destroy it.

Garuda

Swan Maiden

The Swan Maiden is a magnificent swan that turns into a beautiful young woman—stories about this transformation can be found in both Eastern and European sources.

One Eastern version is told in *The Book of One Thousand and One Nights*. Hasan of Basra visits the palace of the bird maidens; when they take off their feathered garments, they transform into beautiful women. Hasan hides the clothes of one to keep her as his wife, but the girl regains her feathers and flies away. After an arduous quest and many adventures, Hasan regains her.

In a Norse version of this story, Völundr, the blacksmith god, marries a Swan Maiden with whom he has a son, but his swan wife escapes, leaving a magical ring in her place.

In Hindu mythology, the Swan Maiden is Saraswati, goddess of music, writing, and inspiration. Ancient images show her seated on a swan or riding through the air on its back.

Mother Goose

Mother Goose is the legendary author of the well-known 19th-century collection of English-language nursery rhymes. On many book covers, she is depicted as a crone-like woman with a long pointed nose and chin wearing a witch's hat and cape. Other book covers show her as a literal goose surrounded by goslings.

Though the illustrators who created these images may not have been aware of their history, the figure of the "Mother" sailing through the air on the back of a goose harkens back to ancient times. As depicted on Greek pottery and in terracotta statues from the 5th century BCE, the Great Mother Aphrodite, mistress of fertility and creativity, rides through the sky with a goose as her mount. Statues of the Mother Goddess as a bird have been dated to the Neolithic period (c. 7000 BCE). Perhaps the popularity of the Mother Goose of the 19th century owes something to its link with these earlier images.

Mother Goose

Lightning Bird

The Lightning Bird is a magical creature to many native peoples of Africa. The real bird most often identified as the Lightning Bird is the Hammerkop. Because of its curved bill and long, shaggy crest, the bird's head resembles a hammer.

Folk beliefs hold that the Lightning Bird appears as a lightning strike. Only women can see the bird in its true form, however; others see only the lightning. The fat of the Lightning Bird is a valuable component in traditional African medicine. To collect it, the bird must be captured at the moment when lightning strikes the ground. Or the bird can be dug up from an underground cavity at the site of the strike, where it lays a large egg. This egg is believed to bring bad luck to the area and must be destroyed. The Lightning Bird is also associated with rain; damaging its nest is thought to bring on a storm.

Jatayu

Jatayu is the huge, semi-divine Vulture King in the Hindu epic, the *Ramayana*. His claws are as long as an elephant tusk and as sharp as iron. He is the son of Aruna, the charioteer of the Sun, and the nephew of Garuda. When Jatayu was young, he competed with his brother bird Sampati to see who could fly higher. Once, when Jatayu flew too near the Sun and nearly scorched his wings, Sampati sheltered him with his own wings, losing them in the process.

In the *Ramayana*, Jatayu, now 60,000 years old, tries to rescue the heroine Sita who has been abducted by the demon Ravana. Though the bird fights valiantly, the demon defeats him. The hero Rama comes upon the dying bird on his own quest to rescue Sita and learns that Sita is alive. A huge rock in the Kerala district of India, said to be the spot where Jatayu died, is an attraction for tourists.

Lightning Bird

Three-legged Bird

The Three-legged Bird is a creature found in the mythologies of China, Japan and Korea. In all three cultures, the bird is thought to live near to or represent the Sun.

In China, the Celestial Cock or Bird of Dawn is envisioned as a three-legged rooster with golden feathers. It nests in a tree that is hundreds of miles high, which grows in the region of the dawn. The ancestor of all the cocks on Earth, its morning crow shakes the sky and awakens humankind.

The Three-legged Bird is a raven called Yatagarasu in Japanese legend. It is the emblem of Amaterasu, the Sun goddess in the Shinto religion. Today, the bird is the emblem of the Japan Football (Soccer) Association.

In Korea, the Three-legged Bird is known as Samjogo. Murals from the ancient Koguryo Kingdom (37 BCE–668 CE) depict the creature as the highest symbol of power, superior to both the Dragon and the Phoenix.

Shang Yang

The Shang Yang, also called the Rain Bird, is a huge one-legged bird in Chinese mythology. It draws water from the rivers with its long, thin beak and blows it out as rain. According to *The Book of Imaginary Beings*, Chinese farmers would call upon the Shang Yang to water their fields. Imitating the bird, children would hop up and down on one leg, wrinkle their foreheads and shout, "It will thunder, it will rain, because the Shang Yang's here again." Once the bird

Three-legged Bird

Shang Yang

flapped its wings and hopped up and down on its single leg before the throne of the Prince of Ch'i. Alarmed, the prince sent his ministers to consult Confucius about the meaning of this portent. The sage foretold that the Shang Yang was about to bring heavy rain and flood the countryside and recommended that dykes and channels be built at once. The prince followed this wise advice and disaster was avoided.

Halcyon

The Halcyon is a bird from Greek mythology renowned for its effect on the weather. Pliny describes the bird as a little larger than a sparrow, sea-blue in color and reddish on the underside, with white feathers at the throat, and a long, slender beak. The real bird most often identified with the Halcyon is the tree kingfisher, a member of the family of kingfishers called Halcyonidae.

The story of the Halcyon is told in many Classical sources, but the most touching version is in Ovid's *Metamorphoses*. King Ceyx of Trachis is married to Alcyone, daughter of Aeolus, the god of winds. Troubled by portents, Ceyx arranges a sea journey to consult an oracle. Terrified of the perils of a sea voyage, Alycone begs her husband not to go or at least to take her along, but Ceyx refuses. Promising to return in two months, he sets sail, leaving Alcyone weeping on the shore.

Soon, his ship is caught up in a terrible mid-winter storm. Despite the best efforts of the mariners, the ship and all hands are lost. Soon after, Alcyone is awakened by a visitation from her husband's shade, who tells her of his death at sea. Alcyone is inconsolable. In the morning, when she wanders grief-stricken to the shore, she sees her husband's corpse washed home by the waves. In despair, she leaps into the sea, but before she reaches the water, she is transformed into a seabird. Her husband, too, transforms, and together the pair nest, mate, and raise their young.

Ever since, for seven days before and seven days after the winter solstice (December 21 in the Northern hemisphere), when the seabirds lay their eggs and hatch their chicks, the ocean is calm and navigable and the winds are quiet, as if Aeolus himself is protecting his daughter and grandchildren. Even today, this mid-winter calm is called the "Halcyon Days."

Halcyon

Insects

THE INSECTS OF WORLD MYTH ARE OFTEN SHAPE-SHIFTERS. SOME WHO
USED TO BE HUMAN BEINGS ARE NOW INSECTS; OTHERS WHO USED TO
BE INSECTS ARE NOW MEN. SOME BECOME MAGICAL CHARMS WHILE
OTHERS ARE EXPERT AT SPINNING WEBS OF MAGICAL DECEPTION.

Itzpapalotl

In the mythology of Aztec Mexico,
Itzpapalotl is a semi-divine butterfly-like
creature. Her name means "Clawed
Butterfly" or "Obsidian Butterfly." Her body
is skeletal, with eagle or jaguar-like claws
and knife-sharp obsidian tips on her
butterfly wings.

To the Aztecs, Itzpapalotl was a
protector of midwives and women in labor.
She was the ruler of Tamoanchan, the
paradise world for babies who die at birth
and home of the Tzitzimimeh, female
fertility figures sometimes described as
"star demons." These beings were associated
with the stars that can be seen during a solar
eclipse. During an eclipse, they were
thought to "attack the Sun" and to descend
to Earth to devour human beings.

In her earthly manifestation, Itzpapalotl
was the leader of the *cihuateteo*, "demons of
the dark"—spirits of women who died
during childbirth. These demons were
believed to haunt crossroads at night,
seducing men and causing illnesses,
especially seizures and madness.

Thriae

The Thriae are three Nymphs in Greek
mythology who possess the gift of
prophecy. Plaques dating back to the 7th
century BCE depict them as having the head
and upper body of a woman and the lower
body and wings of a bee. The head is white,
as if dusted by pollen.

According to a Greek hymn dating to the
7th century BCE, the Thriae lived under a
ridge on Mount Parnassus. There they

taught the art of divination to the young Apollo, god of light, music, and poetry. The food of the Thriae and the source of their poetic gifts is honey, called the "sweet nectar of the gods." Some scholars suggest that the Thriae were human priestesses, who acted as prophetic seers after drinking a honey-laced intoxicant. Others link the Thriae with the Great Mother as the mistress of life, death, and regeneration, pointing to the beehive-shaped tombs at Mycenae dating to 1500 BCE.

Thriae

Tsuchigumo

In Japanese mythology, Tsuchigumo is a fearsome shape-shifting demon in the form of a gigantic, hairy ground spider. It is expert at spinning illusions that draw people into its web so that it can feast on their blood.

Tsuchigumo figures in several tales about the legendary warrior Raiko (948–1021 CE). These tales are retold in a 14th-century Japanese hand scroll and in a traditional Noh play for the Japanese stage. In one, Raiko encounters a mysteriously beautiful woman, who is really Tsuchigumo. She enmeshes Raiko in her web, but the hero wounds her and then kills the spider after a furious battle. In another, Raiko is suffering from a mysterious illness. A monk who comes to pray for him is actually Tsuchigumo in disguise. As the spider spins its web, the warrior wakes up and slashes the beast with his sword. Four of Raiko's retainers follow the spider to its subterranean lair and destroy it, and Raiko recovers.

Tsuchigumo

Arachne

Arachne is the spider woman of Greek mythology. As told in Ovid's *Metamorphoses*, Arachne was a skilled weaver who lived in Lydia. Conceited about her artistry, Arachne boasted that she was more skilled at weaving than Athena, goddess of weaving and crafts.

Athena decided to put this boast to the test by challenging Arachne to a contest. On her loom, Athena wove an exquisite tapestry depicting her competition with Poseidon for the right to be the patron deity of Athens. On hers, Arachne wove scenes of Zeus —Athena's father—transforming into a swan, a bull, and other forms to seduce his human lovers. Outraged at the girl's disrespectful presumption, Athena tore Arachne's tapestry to pieces and destroyed her loom. Then she touched Arachne's forehead with her spindle, making the girl realize her folly. Ashamed, Arachne hanged herself. But Athena took

Illustration showing Arachne challenging Athena.

pity on the girl and transformed the noose into a web and Arachne into a spider—a perpetual and exquisite weaver.

Ant-lion

Ant-lion

The Ant-lion is an impossible creature described in bestiaries. According to *Physiologus*, the Ant-lion's father is a lion and its mother is an ant. Its head and front body resemble its lion father, while its back parts are those of its ant mother.

Because the Ant-lion's father is a meat-eater and its mother is vegetarian, the Ant-lion perishes soon after birth because no food suits its dual nature!

Later bestiaries discarded this description as too preposterous to credit. Instead they said that the creature is called an ant-lion because it hides in the sand and preys like a lion on other ants, sucking the juices from their bodies and robbing them of their winter grain stores. This description led naturalists to use the term "ant-lion" to describe a species of neuroptera larvae. It buries its body in a tunnel of sand, leaving its open mouth above the surface to feed on insects that fall into the tunnel.

Myrmidons

The ant warriors or Myrmidons were the soldiers of the Greek hero Achilles in the Trojan War. Their origin is a curious tale of animal transformation.

According to Greek myth, the island of Aegina was struck by a terrible plague that killed dogs, cattle, sheep, and birds as well as most of the people on the island. In despair, Aegina's King Aeacus prayed to Zeus at a sacred oak tree asking the god to give him back his people. In reply, a clap of thunder shook the tree. That night, the king dreamed of an army of ant warriors. The next morning, he watched in wonder as a multitude of grain-gathering ants grew larger and larger, discarded their superfluous legs, stood erect, and became human beings. Delighted, the king made offerings of thanks to Zeus and allotted his vacant city and fields to his diligent and industrious new subjects, whom he named Myrmidons, from *myrmex*, which means "ant."

Scarab

The Scarab was an important symbol in the religion of ancient Egypt. Scarabs are a kind of dung-beetle, a species that drops its eggs into the ground and covers them with its excrement on which the larvae feed.

As the adult beetles roll the dung ball across the ground with their hind legs, the ball grows in size as dust and sand attach to it. This behavior prompted ancient Egyptians to associate the Scarab with Khepri, the Sun god, who rolls the disc of the Sun across the sky each day and then buries it in the sands.

Symbol of the Sun

The sacred significance of the Scarab was reinforced by its name. Mistakenly, the Egyptians believed that all Scarabs were male and that they reproduced by depositing their semen into the dung ball. The Egyptian word for dung-beetle is *hpr*, which can be translated as "to come into being by itself," "to transform," or "to become." This word reminded Egyptians of the rising Sun, which comes into being by itself each morning, and also of the hope of resurrection and transformation after death.

Amulets carved in the shape of Scarabs were a magical charm commonly worn on a cord. They were believed to protect the wearer from evil influences and provide benefits and blessings. Scarab amulets were carved from semi-precious stones, including carnelian, lapis lazuli, malachite, turquoise, and alabaster. Scarabs inscribed with magical charms and symbols also adorned jewelry, such as pendants, bracelets, necklaces, and rings and were used as official seals on ancient documents.

Heart Scarabs were amulets placed on the throat, chest, or over the heart of a mummy in the hope that the deceased person's heart would not bear witness against him when his actions were judged after death. Heart Scarabs for important mummies were made of green stones, such as jasper and serpentine, set in gold; both the green color and the gold were symbols of resurrection.

Scarab amulet

PART THREE

Creatures from the Shadow World

Monsters of the dark

PEOPLE HAVE ALWAYS BEEN FASCINATED BY GHOULIES, GHOSTIES, AND
OTHER THINGS THAT GO BUMP IN THE NIGHT. FROM THE TALES TOLD
AROUND THE CAMPFIRES IN NEOLITHIC CAVES TO THE BEDTIME STORIES
READ TO CHILDREN IN COZY NURSERIES AROUND THE WORLD,
CREATURES FROM THE SHADOW WORLD HAVE TERRIFIED AND
DELIGHTED US IN EQUAL MEASURE.

Monstrous creatures fascinate us for a
number of reasons. First, they allow us to
tell stories about natural forces we do not
understand and cannot control. Many of the
creatures in this section are linked to
natural forces that challenged the survival
of our ancestors, such as violent storms,
wild beasts, or icy cold. The phantom black
dogs of English folklore often appear during
lightning storms. The Wendigo of Native
American lore possessed people who were
tempted to eat human flesh as a result of
famine or winter cold.

Other creatures speak to fears about our
own bodily processes, including birth,
sexuality, and especially death. Demons that
prey on pregnant women such as the

Kapre

178

Hag

Manananggal from the Philippines, sexual predators that seduce or rape in the night such as the Popobawa of Zanzibar, and animated corpses such as Vampires and Zombies express our terror of the physical body and its powers. Our fears about the end of life are encapsulated in creatures such as the Irish Banshee, whose keening cry announces that someone is about to die.

Monsters also express our fears of the aberrant and the unknown. Many of the creatures in this section are frightening because they lie outside the boundaries of the ordinary. Giants shock because they are so large; Ogres terrify because they are so ugly. But even more frightening, perhaps, are the monsters that may be neighbors we do not know very well. During the day, Japanese Nukekubi look like normal human beings, but at night, their heads and necks detach and fly around looking for people to devour.

Were creatures

FOLKLORE THE WORLD OVER TELLS OF PEOPLE WHO TRANSFORM INTO
A WOLF OR ANOTHER BEAST PURPOSELY BY USING MAGIC, IN
CONSEQUENCE OF THEIR SINS OR BECAUSE THEY HAVE BEEN BEWITCHED
BY OTHERS. THE WORD "WEREWOLF" COMBINES *WERE*, AN OLD ENGLISH
WORD FOR "MAN," AND THE NAME OF THE ANIMAL INTO WHICH THE
PERSON TRANSFORMS, SUCH AS A WOLF, CAT, TIGER, OR BOAR.

Werewolf

Ovid tells the story of the first Werewolf from Greek mythology. Hearing that humankind had become evil, Zeus comes down to the world as a man. When he visits the palace of Lycoan, the king of Arcadia, his host serves him a dish of human flesh. In disgust, Zeus strikes Lycoan with a bolt of lightning, turning him into a bloodthirsty wolf with shaggy hair, red eyes, and a fierce human face.

In medieval Europe, stories about Werewolf transformations were told in many cultures. The English writer Gervase of Tilbury (c.1150–1228 CE) linked the transformation into a Werewolf with the Full Moon. In Russian lore, a child born on

Woodcut of Werewolf

Werewolf

December 24 would become a Werewolf. In Portugal, the seventh son of a family was often named "Bento," which means "blessed," to prevent him from becoming a Werewolf later in life. In Armenia, a sinful woman was said to spend seven years as a child-devouring she-wolf.

In 12th century France, a narrative poem written by Marie de France tells the story of Bisclavret, an unfortunate baron in Brittany, who, for three days of every week, was transformed into a Werewolf. When Bisclavret's faithless wife learned that her husband needed his human clothes to return to human form, she urged her lover to steal the baron's clothes, thus trapping Bisclavret in wolf form. But the noble Bisclavret wins the trust of the king, takes a Werewolf's revenge on his wife by biting off her nose and is at last restored to human form.

Skin-walkers

In Norse and Native American legend, a Skin-walker is a person with the magical power to transform into a wolf, coyote, bear, fox, or other animal—in other words, inhabits the skin of another creature.

In Norse sagas, bands of fierce warriors were said to wear wolf or bear pelts into battle instead of armor. The army of King Harald Fairhair (c.850–933 CE), the first king of Norway, included a group of fighters called *Ulfhednar*, meaning "men clad in wolfskins," who fought with wolf-like fury. The Berserkers—the word means "bear's skin"—were bearskin-clad Norse warriors reputed to be as strong as bears who could kill people with a single blow. The father of a famous Berserker in an Icelandic saga was said to be a werewolf who attacked enemies with his teeth.

Legendary Native American warriors were also said to transform into animals by wearing the pelts of a bear, coyote, wolf, or other animal. The Navajo tradition tells of another kind of Skin-walker, the *Yea-Naagloo-shee*, which means "he goes on all fours." Originally human witches or shamans, these beings gained their evil powers by breaking a cultural taboo. Naked, except for a coyote or wolf pelt or mask, the *Yea-Naa-gloo-shee* would break into homes and attack the people inside. They used magic arts to imitate human voices and would lure people out of the safety of their homes; they were also said to be able to read people's thoughts and would use people's hair, nail clippings, or old clothes to attack them with curses.

A related Cajun legend tells of the Rougarou, a Skin-walker who possessed a human body and the head of a wolf or a dog and prowled the swamps around New Orleans, Louisiana. The name *rougarou* is a variant of *loup-garou*, French for "werewolf." Rougarou stories are often told to frighten children into behaving, although the beast is also said to hunt down Catholics who break the rules of Lent.

Bearskin Warrior

Black dogs

THROUGHOUT EUROPE, LEGENDARY LARGE BLACK DOGS HAVE
APPEARED TO HAUNT PARTICULAR PLACES AND TO PREY ON HUMANS.
SOME ARE AS ANCIENT AS CERBERUS WHILE OTHERS HAVE MORE
RECENT ORIGINS. MANY PARTS OF BRITAIN HAVE REPORTED SIGHTINGS
OF MALEVOLENT BLACK DOGS AND IN BELGIUM A KLUDDE IS SAID TO
ATTACK LONE TRAVELERS.

Phantom black dogs

These creatures are part of the folklore of almost every county in England and Belgium has its own version. Though there are regional variations, most black dogs are said to be as large as a calf, with red eyes as big as saucers, and a shaggy coat. They haunt ancient track ways, crossroads, churchyards, and gallows sites—places associated with superstitions and uncanny events.

Some black dogs are said to appear during electrical storms. A weather vane in Bungay Market, Suffolk, features the image of a black dog known as Black Shuck and a bolt of lightning. On Sunday, August 4, 1577, when St. Mary's church was filled with worshippers, a terrifying thunderstorm shook the building. Suddenly a huge black dog lit by flashes of lightning appeared in the church and attacked many people with its claws and teeth. Most witnesses believed that the beast was a hellhound, an emissary of the devil.

Barghest and Mauthe

In some locales, black dogs are believed to be portents of death. One such creature, called the Barghest, haunts remote places in northern England, especially Yorkshire. It was believed that those who saw the creature clearly would die soon after, while those who caught only a glimpse might live for a few months before succumbing. A similar creature called the Mauthe Dog is said to haunt the guardhouse of the ancient castle of Peel on the Isle of Man. To prove his bravery, a drunken trooper once entered the guardhouse alone, but he lost his speech and died within three days.

Kludde

The black dog of Belgian folklore is called the Kludde. Though the monster usually appears as a giant dog, it can also appear as a cat, frog, bat, or horse. In all forms, it can be identified by the sound of rattling chains and by the blue flame that flickers around its head. The Kludde jumps on to the backs of travelers on lonely roads and mauls them with its teeth and claws.

Phantom black dog

Cerberus

Cerberus

The mythic ancestor of the black dogs of European folklore is Cerberus, the monstrous hellhound that guards the gates of the Underworld in Greek mythology.

Cerberus makes sure that no living person can enter the Underworld and likewise, guarantees that no spirit of the dead can escape. As described in the works of Homer and Hesiod in the 8th century BCE, Cerberus is immensely huge and fierce. Hesiod says the beast has 50 heads and is an offspring of Echidna, the mother of all monsters and Typhon, the final son of Gaia. Later writers and most ancient Greek art depict Cerberus with three heads, the tail of a serpent and a mane with the heads of various snakes.

Cerberus is overcome several times in Greek myth. In order to enter the Underworld, Orpheus lulls Cerberus to sleep with sweet music, Psyche drugs the three-headed creature with honey cakes, and Hermes gives it a drink of water from Lethe, the river of forgetfulness. As his final (12th) labor, the Greek hero Hercules wrestles Cerberus into submission.

Beast of Gévaudan

Some black dog legends have some basis in real-life events. Between 1764 and 1767, a mysterious wolf-like creature is supposed to have attacked and killed between 60 and 100 people in south-central France. Called the Beast of Gévaudan, the creature was as large as a cow, with a wide chest, a long tail ending in a lion-like tuft of fur, large, pointed ears, and a huge mouth with protruding fangs. Locals believed that the creature was a Werewolf or a sorcerer who had shape-shifted into a monster to feed on human flesh.

The beast's method of attack was particularly terrifying. It often targeted the head of its victim, crushing or removing it. It also seemed to prefer human prey, especially women and children, rather than farm animals. Though French King Louis XV sent his best wolf hunters against the beast, it was brought down by a local hunter, Jean Chastel, who claimed to have prayed and read the Bible before his success.

Vampires

VAMPIRES ARE UNDEAD CREATURES WHO LIVE BY SUCKING THE LIFE FORCE FROM OTHERS. THE MOST FAMILIAR TYPE OF VAMPIRE——A SPECTRAL FIGURE IN A BLACK CAPE——COMES FROM EASTERN EUROPE, AND HAS APPEARED IN POPULAR NOVELS AND FILMS. THE MOST FAMOUS OF THESE, BRAM STOKER'S *DRACULA* (1897), MAY HAVE BEEN BASED ON THE 15TH-CENTURY ROMANIAN PRINCE VLAD III THE IMPALER, WHO IS REMEMBERED FOR THE CRUEL PUNISHMENTS IMPOSED DURING HIS REIGN. HOWEVER, MYTHS SURROUNDING VAMPIRES ARE FOUND ALL OVER THE WORLD, FROM EASTERN EUROPE TO INDIA, AUSTRALIA, AND THE AMERICAS.

Vampire

Eastern European Vampires

In eastern European legends, Vampires are animated corpses that rise from the grave to prey on the living. Vampires attack by biting living victims' necks to drink their blood. The corpses of suicide victims, criminals, or sorcerers may become Vampires, though in some traditions, innocent victims of Vampire attacks become Vampires themselves. Babies born with teeth, a lot of

Woodcut showing Vlad Tepes dining among the impaled.

hair, or a missing finger or toe are also likely to become Vampires.

Folk remedies to ward off Vampire attacks are as famous as the creatures themselves. To kill a Vampire, cut off its head, drive a stake through its heart, or burn the corpse. To prevent a corpse from becoming a Vampire, drive a hawthorn stake through the body to pin it to the ground or place a scythe across the neck so that the corpse is decapitated if it tries to rise. Vampires also fear garlic and Christian symbols such as crosses and holy water. On the eves of the feasts of St. George and St. Andrew, when Vampires are especially active, people in eastern Europe sprinkled holy water around their homes and rubbed their cattle with garlic.

In the early 18th century, a Vampire panic gripped East Prussia and Austria-Hungary. A Serbian farmer, for instance, who was believed to have become a Vampire was blamed for a number of rural deaths. The government investigated and laws were passed to prohibit the opening of graves and the desecration of bodies.

Vampires around the world

Legends about Vampires are among the most persistent and widespread folk beliefs, and can be found in cultures the world over. The consistent theme running through most of the myths is the idea of undead or spirit creatures consuming the life force, flesh, or blood of the living.

Greek Vampires

Known as *Vrylolakas* in Greece, Vampires are believed to be the spirit of a deceased person who has not been properly mourned or whose body has not been given the proper rites—the spirit might linger around the corpse and reanimate it. As recently as the early 20th century, corpses were exhumed and examined after three years to make sure the body was decayed. If the corpse was stiff and swollen "like a drum," the person was believed to have become a Vampire.

Chinese Vampires

In China, Vampires are called "hopping corpses" or Jiang Shi, which means "stiff corpse." The name comes from a practice detailed in Chinese folklore whereby a family who could not afford to travel to the place where a relative died to bring back the body would hire a Taoist priest to animate the corpse so that it could hop back home for burial. In contemporary Chinese Vampire movies, a Jiang Shi can be put to sleep by putting a piece of yellow paper on its forehead on which a spell is written.

American Vampires

In the United States in 1892, the body of 19-year-old tuberculosis victim Mercy Brown, who died in Exeter, Rhode Island, was exhumed two months after her death. Since her body was not decomposed and she had liquid blood in her heart, it was feared that she had become a Vampire who was infecting others with her illness. Her heart was removed and burned, and its ashes were mixed with water and fed to her gravely ill brother, but the boy died two months later.

Presidental Vampires

In Pozarevac, Serbia in March 2007, self-proclaimed Vampire hunters broke into the tomb of Slobodan Milosevic, the infamous former president of Serbia and Yugoslavia. The vandals drove a 3-feet-long (1 meter) wooden stake through his heart and into the ground to keep the much-despised leader from returning from the dead to haunt the country.

Jiang Shi

Vetala

Hindu and Australian Vampires

In Hindu folklore, a Vetala is a Vampire-like spirit that haunts cemeteries and inhabits corpses in order to move around; another type of Vampire is the Yara-ma-yha-who of Australia, a little red man who sucks his victim's blood through his sucker-like hands and feet.

Vetala

Since this hostile spirit lacks a body, it animates the dead in order to attack the living. Vetalas are said to cause madness and miscarriages, and to kill children. Because they live in the realm between life and death, Vetalas can see the past, present, and future and for this reason, magicians try to enslave them. Ordinary people can ward off Vetala attacks by chanting prayers and mantras.

An ancient sorcerer, according to legend, asked King Vikramaditya to capture a Vetala that lived in a tree that stood near the kingdom's cremation grounds. To succeed, the king had to remain silent. But every time he captured the Vetala, the creature told the king a magical story ending in a question. No matter how hard he tried to keep quiet, the king was compelled to answer the question. When the king spoke, the Vetala escaped and returned to his tree.

Australian Yara-ma-yha-who

The Vampire of Indigenous Australian culture is the Yara-ma-yha-who, a little red man just over 3-feet (1 meter) tall with a large head and a gaping mouth. The Yara-ma-yha-who lives at the top of fig trees, holding on with fingers and toes that resemble the suckers of an octopus.

When an unsuspecting person takes shelter under an inhabited fig tree, the Yara-ma-yha-who jumps down and sucks the person's blood with its hands and feet, leaving the victim weak and helpless, but rarely causing death. Later, the creature comes back to swallow the person whole. After a nap, it regurgitates the undigested part of its meal. The consumed person is still alive, though a little shorter than before, after they have been eaten!

Philippines and Central American Vampires

The Manananggal of the Philippines takes the form of a woman while the Central American Vampire-like creature has a somewhat reptilian appearance.

Manananggal

The Vampire of the Philippines is the Manananggal, a creature that looks like an older but very beautiful woman. Each night, she separates her torso in two at the waist—the word *manananggal* means "self-remover" in Tagalog—leaves her lower body behind and flies off on huge, bat-like wings to seek her prey. Her favorite victims are pregnant women sleeping peacefully in their homes. Using her elongated proboscis-like tongue, she sucks out the heart of the fetus or the blood of the unsuspecting mother-to-be.

When she flies away, the lower half of a Manananggal's body is left standing. Several folk remedies can prevent the two halves from reattaching, including sprinkling the lower torso with salt or smearing it with crushed garlic. If the Manananggal cannot rejoin her severed body by daybreak, she will die. Men who have been seduced by the Manananggal stand guard over her lower body to keep it safe for her return.

Chupacabra

In parts of the Americas, the Chupacabra—the word means "goat sucker"—has been blamed for attacks on livestock, especially goats. People who have seen the creature describe it as being about 3-feet (1 meter) high, with leathery, greenish-gray skin, a row of sharp spines down its back, protruding fangs, and a forked tongue. It is said to hop on its hind legs like a kangaroo, to hiss or screech when alarmed, and to emit a sulphuric stench.

First reported in Puerto Rico in 1990, the creature attacks animals by drinking their blood through a series of small, circular incisions. Many people believe that the Chupacabra is an unknown or alien species with supernatural powers. Reports claim that it can hypnotize an animal with its eyes allowing it to suck the blood of its prey through its hollow fangs.

Chupacabra

Sexual predators

SOME VAMPIRE-LIKE BEINGS ARE SEXUAL PREDATORS. INCUBI AND
SUCCUBI APPEARED AS EARLY AS 3000 BCE, AND LAMIA, FROM GREEK
MYTHOLOGY, CONSORTED WITH THE GODS. EVEN TODAY, THERE ARE
MYTHS SURROUNDING SIMILAR CREATURES IN THE FORM OF
POPOBAWA IN ZANZIBAR.

Incubus and Succubus

An Incubus is a male demon who attacks women, usually while they are lying in bed, raping them or arousing them to welcome sexual intercourse. The victim does not awaken, though she may experience the encounter in her dreams. The female counterpart of the Incubus is the Succubus.

Unlike the Incubus, who looks like a hideous demon in most European medieval drawings, the Succubus is a beautiful and desirable woman, though she sometimes has bat-like wings or demonic features such as horns, a tail, hooves, and fangs.

The earliest instance of Incubi and Succubi is found in the mythology of ancient Sumeria around 3000 BCE. The Lilitu were nocturnal storm and wind spirits who were highly sexual and predatory. The father of the hero Gilgamesh is said to be Lilu, an Incubus-like spirit.

Medieval demons

In medieval European lore, Succubi appeared to men in the night and seduced them into sexual encounters. Celibate monks seemed to be especially prone to such attacks, often blaming Succubi for their lustful thoughts or sexual dreams. Succubi could suck the life force of men, leaving them exhausted or even killing them. Incubi could possess men and force them to become sexual predators. According to the *Malleus Maleficarum* (1486), a medieval treatise on witchcraft, possession or attacks could be prevented by

Succubus

religious rituals such as confession, making the sign of the cross, excommunication, and exorcism.

According to early Christian writers, because demons were unable to reproduce by ordinary means, an Incubus would transform into a Succubus to gather semen from human men, which they used to impregnate human women. The children born from such unions were said to possess supernatural powers or to be susceptible to demonic influence. Merlin, the sorcerer in the legends of King Arthur, was reputed to be the child of a human mother and a demon-lover.

Lamia

In Greek mythology, Lamia was a female demon who seduced sleeping men and devoured children. Descriptions of the creature vary; some say she was a beautiful woman above the waist and a hideous serpent below. Medieval bestiaries depicted her as having the face of a beautiful woman but the body of a goat, with cloven hooves and a hide covered with rainbow-hued scales like a dragon.

According to one version of her story, the original Lamia was a beautiful queen of Libya who was loved by Zeus, king of the gods. Hera, the jealous queen of the gods, kidnapped and murdered Lamia's children to take revenge for the affair. Lamia's despair drove her mad and she retreated to a cave, where her rage transformed her into a hideous demon who snatched up and murdered children by sucking their blood. Other stories say that she could regain her beauty and transform into a night monster that preyed sexually on men.

Popobawa

Sexually predatory night monsters are still terrorizing people in parts of the world. According to news reports, modern-day men on the Zanzibar islands often sleep in groups beside a huge fire outside their homes or smear themselves with pig's oil to repel attacks by the Popobawa (meaning "bat-wing").

This male demon with bat-like talons, wings and a single evil-looking eye attacks and rapes men when they are sleeping alone in their own beds. In 1995, a series of reported attacks caused widespread panic in the region.

The creature reveals its presence by an acrid smell and a puff of smoke. Victims report that immediately before the sexual attack, they experience paralysis and the sensation of something pressing on their chests, making them feel as if they are suffocating. Some believe that the creature is a vengeful vestige of the horrors of the slave market that existed on Zanzibar during the mid-19th century.

Lamia

Dead creatures

DEAD CREATURES INCLUDE REANIMATED HUMAN CORPSES SUCH AS
ZOMBIES, MESSENGERS OF DEATH LIKE THE BANSHEE, AND ANIMATED
ARTIFICIAL CREATURES SUCH AS THE GOLEM.

Zombies

Versions of Zombies appear in the folklore of world cultures dating back to prehistory. When the mythological hero Gilgamesh spurns the advances of the goddess Ishtar, she threatens to take revenge by allowing the dead to "go up and eat the living." Since that time, fears of corpses attacking the living have been part of the folk beliefs of many lands.

In France during the Middle Ages, it was believed that a person who had been murdered might rise from the grave to avenge the crime.

In England, 12th-century historian William of Newburgh described several cases of reanimated corpses—or revenants—hideous creatures that wandered through villages at night spreading disease and killing anyone they met.

Draugr

In Norse mythology, the Draugr were the corpses of Viking warriors returned from the dead to attack the living. As Viking warriors were likely to be buried with valuable weapons and other wealth, the Draugr guarded the grave's treasures much like a Dragon protecting its hoard. The Draugr were believed to have supernatural strength and to be able to grow to giant size after they emerged from the grave as wisps of smoke. These creatures killed living beings by crushing them, devouring them or drinking their blood.

Vodou

In the Caribbean republic of Haiti, practitioners of Vodou (voodoo) believe that a Bokor or sorcerer can revive a corpse, creating a Zombie who remains under the

Bokor's power. Others say that Vodou sorcerers can turn living people into Zombies by introducing a drug made from the poison of a pufferfish into their bloodstreams through a wound. The drug induces a trance-like state in which the person becomes the slave of the Bokor.

Zombies in fiction

Zombies appear as "monsters" in popular books dating back to Mary Shelley's *Frankenstein* (1818) and films such as George A. Romero's *Night of the Living Dead* (1968).

Draugr

Banshee

In Celtic mythology, the Banshee—from Irish meaning "the woman of the Sidhe" or fairy world—is a female messenger spirit and an omen of death.

A Banshee is generally dressed in white or gray robes. She may be combing her long, fair hair with a silver comb or else washing the bloodstains from the clothes of the person who is about to die. She announces her presence by keening—a wailing cry so piercing that it can shatter glass.

According to Irish folk beliefs, when a member of one of Ireland's noble families is about to die, a Banshee appears to announce the death. In 1642, Lady Fanshaw, made famous as the "Lady of the Lake" in the poem of the same title by Sir Walter Scott, was awakened in the night by a ghostly apparition keening outside her window when she was visiting a baronial castle. In the morning, she discovered that a member of the baron's family had died in the night.

Banshee

202

Golem

In Jewish folklore, a Golem is an animated artificial man. The word "golem" comes from the Hebrew word *gelem*, which means "raw material."

Traditionally, a Golem was fabricated from clay and animated by having a magical or religious word written on its forehead or on a piece of parchment placed in its mouth. A Golem with the Hebrew word *Emet* (truth) on its forehead could be deactivated by erasing the first letter to form the word *Met* (death).

There are many tales in which medieval European rabbis, following instructions given in the mystical Kabbalistic text, the *Sefer Yetzirah*, created and animated Golems to do their bidding. The most famous of these was created by Rabbi Judah Loew, a leading 16th-century scholar in Prague. According to legend, Rabbi Loew created a Golem to protect the residents of Prague's Jewish ghetto from harm. But the creature turned violent and began killing non-Jews before turning on its creator.

Golem

Giants

BEINGS OF IMMENSE SIZE HAVE APPEARED IN WORLD FOLKLORE FROM
EARLIEST TIMES. GIANTS PLAY A CENTRAL ROLE IN THE CREATION
MYTH OF MANY CULTURES—SOME TELL THAT THE WORLD WAS
FORMED FROM THE BODY OF A DEFEATED OR DISMEMBERED GIANT,
WHILE OTHERS RECOUNT A WAR BETWEEN A RACE OF GIANTS AND THE
GODS, WHICH MADE IT POSSIBLE FOR HUMANKIND TO EXIST.

Famous Giants

Name	Culture	Background	Mythology
Nephilim	Middle East	Evil Giants from Genesis said to be the offspring of human women and fallen angels, giving them superhuman strength	Their wickedness, vice, and sexual promiscuity were among the reasons God sent the Great Flood
Atlas	Greek	One of the powerful Titans defeated by Zeus and the Olympian gods	Condemned by Zeus to stand at the western edge of the Earth and hold the celestial globe of the sky on his shoulders
Pan Gu	Chinese	Primitive Giant with horns on his head, clad in furs, central to the Chinese creation myth	With a swing of his giant axe, he separated the yin and yang of the Cosmic Egg, creating the Earth and the sky

Balor of the Evil Eye	Celtic	One-eyed king of the Fomorians, a Giant and monstrous race who were ancient inhabitants of Ireland	His single eye killed anyone it looked upon; four men using a handle fitted to the eyelid opened it on the battlefield
Gogmagog	British	Leader of a race of gigantic humanoid beings who lived in prehistoric Britain	Defeated by the Trojan warrior Corrineus, who threw him from the top of the Cornish cliffs
Ymir	Norse	Founder of the race of Frost Giants and central to the Norse creation myth	His skull became the sky, his flesh became the earth, his blood formed seas and lakes, his teeth and bones became mountains
Daityas	Hindu	Giant evil spirits who warred with the gods during the first age of the Cosmos	Defeated by a divine army led by the goddess Indra, who imprisoned them in the depths of the ocean
Purusha	Hindu	Primordial Giant with 1,000 heads and 1,000 feet	Dismembered, his mind became the Moon, his eyes became the Sun and his breath became the wind
Zipacna	Mayan	Arrogant and demonic Giant who boasted that he had created the mountains	Defeated by divine Hero Twins who caused a mountain to collapse on him
Jentilak	Basque	Race of pre-Christian Giants who lived in the western Pyrenees of Spain and France	Raised the dolmens and menhirs (standing stones) by tossing gigantic rocks from one mountain to another

Titans and Gigantes

In the earliest layer of Greek mythology, the Titans were powerful beings who ruled the world during the Golden Age, while the Gigantes were sometimes depicted as Greek warriors and at others as primitives.

Titans

Many Titans were identified with natural forces, including Uranus, who represents Heaven and Gaia, who represents Earth. Fearing the power of his children, Uranus trapped them in Gaia's womb until his youngest son Cronus, who represents Time, overthrew his father, castrating him and spreading his seed on the fertile earth.

Cronus set himself up as the new chief god, with Rhea as his queen. A second generation of powerful Titans was born from this union. Fearing that he, too, would be overthrown by his offspring, Cronus swallowed each child whole. But Rhea tricked him, giving him a stone wrapped in swaddling clothes rather than the infant Zeus. When he reached adulthood, Zeus conspired with his grandmother Gaia to concoct a potion that caused his father

to vomit up his siblings who then became the first generation of Olympian gods. Led by Zeus, the Olympians went to war against the mighty Titans, overthrowing them and imprisoning many in the Underworld.

Gigantes

But the Olympians, too, faced a challenge to their sovereignty. The seed of Cronus had fertilized the earth, which brought forth a race of Giants called the Gigantes. To reach the gods in their stronghold at the top of Mount Olympus, the Gigantes stacked rocks on each other, creating the mountain ranges of mainland Greece.

The war between the Olympians and the Gigantes is a favorite theme of Greek artists. Some depict the Gigantes as Greek warriors wearing armor and carrying

The Titans challenge the gods, but are defeated.

spears; others see them as primitives wearing panther skins and armed with rocks. Many vase paintings and mosaics show the Gigantes with serpent tails instead of legs. The defeat of the Gigantes, with the aid of the hero Hercules, made the world safe for human habitation; however, buried deep within the earth, the Gigantes are blamed for earthquakes and volcanic eruptions.

Ancient and modern Giants

Giants from the Judeo-Christian, Norse, and Celtic traditions live alongside more modern stories of a giant from American folklore.

Jotun

The Giants of Norse mythology are the Jotun, offspring of the primordial Giant Ymir, from whose body the world was formed. The Jotun represent the forces of chaos and the untamed and destructive powers of nature. The Jotun and the Norse gods, led by Odin, are perpetually at war. Victories by the gods symbolize the triumph of culture and civilization over raw nature. However, this war requires constant vigilance. At the end of time, the final battle, Ragnarök—the twilight of the gods —will take place. The Fire Giants will set fire to Yggdrasil, the world tree, all living creatures will perish in the conflagration and the Universe will be destroyed.

Goliath

The battle between the youth David and the giant Goliath is told in Judeo-Christian texts and the Islamic Koran. In the 11th century BCE, the Israelites led by King Saul were at war with the Philistines who had invaded the southern coast of Canaan. In some versions, Goliath's height is given as "four cubits and a span" (about 7 feet/ 2 meters); other sources say that he stood 10 feet (3 meters) tall.

Each day, Goliath challenged the Israelites to send a champion against him. The Israelites were afraid, except for David who convinced Saul to allow him to face the Giant. Armed only with his sling and smooth stones, David invoked the power of God and felled Goliath with a single stone. Taking up the Giant's sword, he cut off his head, causing the Philistine army to flee in dismay.

Unlike most other artistic depictions, the famous marble statue by Michelangelo (1504) shows David before his battle with Goliath, his muscles tensed for combat.

David and Goliath

Fomorians

The first mythological invaders of Ireland are the Fomorians whose king is the one-eyed Giant Balor of the Evil Eye. Like the Norse Jotun, the Fomorians represent the dark chaos of nature. Some have human bodies and horses' heads; others have scales like fish and flippers instead of feet. An 11th-century text says that some have one eye, one arm, and one leg. A few, however, look like beautiful humans. The dark Fomorians are at war with the race of younger gods, the Tuatha De Danann—Elf-like beings that represent the forces of light. Their leader Lugh is the son of Balor's daughter Eithne, imprisoned by her father because of a prophecy that her son will kill him. Lugh's father is the Tuatha lord, Cian. Like the young David, Lugh fights Balor with a slingshot, striking Balor's single eye, driving it back into his head so that its lethal gaze is turned against his own army.

Paul Bunyan

Not all giants are malicious. A famous Giant from American folklore is Paul Bunyan, a lumberjack of colossal size and titanic strength—his footsteps created 10,000 lakes in the state of Minnesota. Paul also dug the Grand Canyon in Arizona by dragging his axe behind him and built Oregon's Mount Hood by piling rocks on top of a campfire to put it out. His blue ox Babe is similarly gargantuan, measuring 42 axe handles wide between its massive horns.

Stories about Paul and Babe were told around the campfires in lumber camps during the 19th century. Paul's larger-than-life adventures, in which he overcomes nights so cold that the flames in the lanterns freeze solid and mosquitoes so big they need a runway to land, symbolize the rugged vitality of the American frontiersman, who can overcome all obstacles through courage and hard work.

Paul Bunyan

Grendel and his mother

Grendel and his mother

An early Anglo-Saxon epic features the Giant Grendel and his mother, the monstrous opponents of Beowulf, hero of the narrative poem composed in England during the early Middle Ages (c.750–1000 CE). The events of the poem took place in Scandinavia during the late 5th and early 6th centuries when Anglo-Saxon tribes had begun to migrate and settle in England, perhaps bringing the Beowulf legends with them.

Though Grendel and his mother are never described clearly in the narrative, they are Giant-like beings with iron-tough skin and jaws powerful enough to crush a man. The two live in an underwater lair, near Heorot, the great feasting hall of King Hroogar. Grendel, an outcast from civilized society, has been terrorizing the assembly, attacking the hall at night, killing and devouring many warriors. Beowulf, a young warrior of the Geat tribe, arrives to offer assistance.

During the night, Grendel attacks the hall and eats one of Beowulf's men. An epic battle takes place, which ends when Beowulf rips off Grendel's arm at the shoulder, and the monster slinks back to his lair to die.

The revenge of Grendel's mother

The next night Grendel's even more monstrous mother attacks the hall and kills a warrior to avenge her son's death. Beowulf and his men track her to an eerie lake. The fight between Beowulf and this fearsome antagonist takes place in the underwater lair. In the end, Beowulf beheads the monster with a sword taken from her own armory, so huge no other human could have used it in battle. For good measure, Beowulf also cuts off Grendel's head and returns to Heorot victorious.

Beowulf's end

Later in life, after he has become king of his people, Beowulf fights his final battle— against a Dragon. Though he succeeds in killing the beast, he is mortally wounded in combat and dies. The treasure of the Dragon he killed is buried with him on a barrow overlooking the sea.

The Troll and the Boy by John Bauer.

Trolls and Ogres

Trolls and Ogres are the mythical Giants of northern European folk and fairy tales, especially those written or collected in the 19th century. Though these creatures resemble the Norse Jotun (see page 208) in some ways, their appearance and attributes are more varied. Some tales depict them as fiendish cannibalistic Giants; others as more human or Dwarf-like creatures who live in the wilderness, often underground in hills, caves, or mounds.

As depicted in Scandinavian folklore, Trolls are generally large, brutish, and ugly, sometimes with beast-like features such as horns, hairy or warty skin, long arms, humpbacks, and oversized ears and noses. Trolls are often described as having low intelligence, though they are devious and steal and hoard human treasures or abduct human babies, substituting one of their own offspring.

In many stories, Trolls are nocturnal creatures and change to stone when they are exposed to sunlight. Some Trolls are shape-shifters and can disguise themselves as rocks, logs or animals. The word "troll" may come from an Old Norse word that means "magic."

Child-eaters

In French and English folk and fairy tales, there is a creature similar to the Troll called an Ogre (or ogress if it is feminine). Like Trolls, Ogres are giant beings with superhuman size and strength, an oversized head, large belly, and long wild hair. But their most terrifying attribute is their liking for a meal of human flesh, especially children. For this reason, they often appear as the monster in children's fairy tales.

Again, like Trolls, Ogres are said to have low intelligence, so they are relatively easy to trick or defeat. Some are also shape-shifters, an attribute that can be used against them. In the classic fairy tale "Puss-in-Boots," the clever cat tricks a shape-shifting Ogre into transforming into a mouse. As soon as the creature complies, Puss-in-Boots pounces on the mouse and devours it.

Demons

THESE CREATURES HOLD SWAY IN MYTH AND LEGEND AROUND THE WORLD, BUT ARE OFTEN SEEN AS SUPERNATURAL BEINGS OF MALEVOLENCE, AND IN SOME CHRISTIAN MYTHOLOGY, DEMONS ARE THOUGHT TO BE FALLEN ANGELS.

Rakshasa

The demon monster of Hindu mythology is the rakshasa. As described in the Hindu epic, the *Ramayana*, Rakshasas come in many shapes and sizes. Some are disgustingly ugly with monstrous bellies, hanging breasts, long projecting teeth, and crooked thighs. Others have three or four legs and the heads of serpents, donkeys, horses, or elephants. They can be very fat or very lean, prodigiously tall or dwarfish, or have only one eye or one ear.

According to legend, Rakshasas were particularly wicked humans who have been reincarnated in monstrous form as a result of their evil deeds. They enjoy disturbing holy rituals and harassing mediators. Cannibals and blood-drinkers, they feed on human flesh, haunt cemeteries, and desecrate graves. They are also gifted magicians and shape-shifters.

Ravana

The king of the Rakshasas is Ravana. In the *Ramayana*, he is described as having ten heads, 20 arms, copper-colored eyes, and a gaping mouth. Other passages describe him as being as tall as a mountain peak and so powerful that he can stir the seas and split the tops of mountains.

As the villain of the *Ramayana*, Ravana transforms himself into an old beggar and kidnaps Sita, the beautiful wife of the hero Rama. Helped by human and animal allies, Rama follows Ravana to the city of Lanka where a furious battle ensues in which the gods Vishnu and Indra fight on Rama's side. The fortunes of combat wax and wane until

Rakshasa

it is decided that the war will be resolved by single combat between Rama and Ravana.

Each time Rama takes off one of Ravana's heads with an arrow, it grows back at once. Finally, Ravana's brother who has defected to Rama's side, tells Rama to shoot at the demon's navel—the source of his powers of regeneration. Taking careful aim, Rama brings down the demon and a rain of heavenly flowers celebrates his victory.

Oni and Yokai

The Oni are the ogres of Japanese folklore —large savage humanoids with demonic features such as red skin or hair, horns and claws, wearing only a loincloth or tiger skin, and carrying a spiked iron club. The Yokai, on the other hand, are seen as less malicious spirits or demons.

In folktales, Oni are malicious, man-eating creatures that must be slain by brave heroes. However, Oni can also serve as protectors. The demon-faced tiles at the end of Japanese roofs are called *onigawara* tiles, because the scowling demons are believed to scare away harmful spirits.

In traditional Japanese culture, villages hold annual ceremonies to drive out the Oni, generally during the Setsuban festival at the beginning of spring. People throw soybeans either out of the door or at a member of the family wearing an Oni mask while shouting, "*Oni wa soto! Fuku wa uchi!*" ("Demons out! Luck in!") The beans are thought to purify the home by driving away evil spirits.

Oni

Mischief-makers

While Oni are almost always malicious, Yokai—the word means "apparitions," "spirits," or "demons"—may be simply bothersome or mischievous:

- **Hitotsume-kozo** (One-eyed boys) are the size of small boys but otherwise resemble bald Buddhist priests with one giant eye in the center of their faces. More annoying than dangerous, they frighten people or tell them to be quiet if they are being too loud.

- **Rokurokubi** also look like normal human beings by day, but at night they can stretch their necks to great lengths and alter their features so that they resemble Oni. Tricksters by nature, they frighten and spy on people rather than attacking them.

- **Nukekubi** look like normal human beings by day, but at night their heads and necks detach from the rest of their bodies and fly around looking for human prey. Before they attack, they scream to increase their victims' fear. To spot a Nukekubi, look for a ring of red symbols around the base of a person's neck.

Kapre and other Filipino demons

The Kapre is a tree demon from the folklore of the Philippines. A hairy, bearded man-like creature, about 7–10 feet (2–3 meters) tall, the Kapre likes tobacco and is generally smoking a pipe or a long cigar.

Kapres dwell in large trees, such as the acacia or banyan. They are wild creatures and wear only a loincloth and a magical belt, which makes them invisible to humans. Kapres are fond of tricks and can confuse travelers so that they become lost in the mountains or woods. In addition to the smell of tobacco or smoke coming from the top of a tree, other signs that a Kapre is nearby include rustling tree branches when the wind is still, loud laughter or a disembodied voice in the woods or an abundance of fireflies.

Sigbin

The Sigbin is a demon that resembles a goat with no horns, but with very large ears that it claps together like hands. It walks backward, with its head lowered between its hind legs. It is especially dangerous during Easter week, when it emerges from its lair seeking the hearts of human victims, preferably children.

Tiyanak

The Tiyanak is a demon that takes the form of a newborn baby crying in the jungle to attract travelers. If the traveler picks up the infant, the creature reverts to its demonic shape and attacks the person with its sharp claws and fangs.

Batibat

The Batibat, like the Kapre, dwells in trees, though it takes the form of a huge, fat woman. If the tree in which it lives is cut down to make the post of a house, the Batibat hides in the posthole and attacks people in the night by sitting on their chests and suffocating them. To escape, a person must bite his thumb or wiggle his toes to awaken.

Kapre

Shape-shifters

THE ABILITY TO SHIFT FROM ONE PHYSICAL FORM TO ANOTHER IS THE
MARK OF A SHAPE-SHIFTER IN THE FOLKLORE AND MYTH OF MANY
CULTURES, FROM THE PHILIPPINES AND NORTH AMERICA TO ANCIENT
CELTIC LEGEND.

Aswang

Another predatory creature in the folklore of the Philippines is the Aswang, a shape-shifter that appears in many guises. A common appearance is as a witch-like woman with leathery wings and bloody fangs, though it may also appear as a dog, bat, or snake.

Aswangs rob graves and eat dead bodies, replacing the corpse with a banana tree trunk carved in the likeness of the dead person. They also feed on small children, particularly savoring their livers and hearts.

Some believe that Aswangs may live among human beings, preferring to work as butchers or sausage-makers. At night, they assume their true appearance. When they stalk their prey on foot, Aswangs walk with their feet facing backward and their toenails reversed. The tail of a stingray, a shiny sword, or a picture of a grandmother are effective weapons against them. Some also believe that throwing salt at an Aswang causes their skin to burn.

Aswang

Wendigo

The Wendigo is a malevolent creature from Native American mythology, specifically the Algonquin people, who were the original inhabitants of northeastern North America.

Wendigos are evil spirits into which human beings can transform, causing them to become cannibalistic monsters. In some depictions, Wendigos are tall, gaunt, and skeletal, with an ash-gray complexion, eyes pushed deep into their sockets and an eerie odor of decay. In others, the creature is a giant beast with fangs and horns who grows larger with each person that it devours.

All Algonquin traditions associate the Wendigo with winter, the north, coldness, famine, and starvation. If a human ever resorted to eating the body of another human being as a result of famine, he was at risk of becoming a Wendigo—a violent and insatiable monster obsessed with eating human flesh. Perhaps stories about the Wendigo served as a cultural deterrent against cannibalism, especially in times of extreme hardship.

Obake and the Kitsune

Japanese folklore includes many kinds of supernatural animal shape-shifters, known collectively as Obake. These beings, which include tanuki (raccoon dogs), hebi (snakes), mujina (badgers), bakeneko (cats), okami (wolves), and tsuchigumo (spiders) range from clever tricksters and ghostly apparitions to terrifying and predatory monsters.

Sometimes all of these attributes are combined in one Obake, as is the case with the Kitsune or fox spirit.

Some Kitsune are wise and benevolent, but others are mischievous or malicious. Kitsune look like ordinary foxes, but may have as many as nine tails. The more tails a Kitsune has, the older and more powerful it is. According to some stories, only a Kitsune that has lived for 1,000 years has nine tails.

A Kitsune that has lived more than 100 years gains the ability to assume human form. Commonly, it places a broad leaf or a skull over its head and transforms into a beautiful young girl or an elderly man.

In medieval Japan, any young woman encountered alone at dusk was feared to be a Kitsune. Human Kitsune often reveal their true nature by being unable to hide their tails or by casting a fox-shaped shadow.

Kitsune possession

Demonic Kitsune can also possess human beings or drive them mad. A Kitsune that seeks to possess a young woman enters her beneath her fingernails or through her breasts. The young woman then begins to look more fox-like and to have a voracious fox-like appetite. She may also run naked shouting through the streets, yelp like a fox, or froth at the mouth.

In other tales, Kitsune have the ability to generate fire from their tails, bend time and space, become invisible, and shape-shift into other terrifying forms such as a gigantic tree or a second moon in the sky. Monstrous Kitsunes may behave like Vampires or Succubi (see pages 188–195 and 196–197), feeding on the life force of living beings through sexual contact.

Kitsune

Kelpie and Each Uisge

These shape-shifting water horses from the folklore of Scotland and Ireland known as Kelpie and Each Uisge (pronounced "ech ooshskya") are similar, although the Kelpie live in freshwater rivers, lakes (lochs), and streams, while the Each Uisge prefer the sea and sea lochs. Though both are dangerous, the Each Uisge is considered more deadly.

The Kelpie usually appears standing near a river or stream looking like a beautiful pony with a grayish black or stark white coat. Its mane is always dripping with water. By appearing to be lost or tame, it lures an unwary traveler to mount it. Then, making a sound like thunder, the Kelpie dives into deep water and drowns the unfortunate rider who is magically stuck to its back. Kelpies are also said to warn of impending storms by wailing and howling.

As a shape-shifter, a Kelpie can also assume human form, which it may do to seduce a human lover. To identify a Kelpie lover, look for a piece of seaweed entwined in the hair. A Kelpie's shape-shifting power is contained in its bridle. Taming a Kelpie by possessing its bridle is dangerous but useful as a captive Kelpie is said to have the strength of ten ordinary horses.

More gruesome

The Each Uisge is not content with drowning its victims. Once a rider has mounted, the creature dives into the water and tears the person apart, devouring the entire body except for the liver. Once, near Aberfeldy, Scotland, seven little girls and a little boy were walking beside the loch when they saw a pony grazing. One by one the girls climbed on its back, which magically expanded to accommodate them. Seeing this, the boy ran away and watched in horror as the pony plunged into the loch. Next morning, the livers of the seven children were washed ashore.

Kelpie

Household spirits

British folklore includes many types of malicious or troublesome household spirits. Almost all are shape-shifters and can manifest in different forms, though most are small and roughly human-shaped, with claws, prominent teeth, or other demonic attributes. Each type has its typical haunts and characteristic behaviors.

Redcap

This murderous little creature haunts ruined castles along the border between England and Scotland. It gets its name from the red cap it wears, which it dyes with the blood of its victims. Redcaps often carry an iron pike and wear iron-shod boots. Travelers who visit the ruins risk being attacked. Though it is impossible to outrun a Redcap, quoting a verse from the Bible may help a person to escape.

Boggart

This household pest is often described as being squat, hairy, and smelly. It can cause objects to disappear, milk to sour, and dogs to go lame. It also delights in frightening people by pulling off their bed sheets at night or placing a clammy hand on their faces. Though Boggarts are said to follow a family wherever it moves, hanging a horseshoe above the door is said to provide some protection.

Boggart

228

Bogle

This malicious creature from Scottish folklore has a fierce temper. It enjoys making trouble for children who are lazy or disobedient. It may create a mess by knocking over the milk jug or make weird noises that are blamed on the children or frustrate them by calling out to them in human voices when there is no one there.

Gremlins

This mechanically oriented creature is said to have haunted and sabotaged aircraft during the Second World War. A 1942 article in the *Royal Air Force Journal* mentions Gremlins as the cause of accidents that occurred during flights. One Air Force crewman swore that he saw creatures tinkering with the engine before a malfunction caused the bomber in which he was flying to lose altitude rapidly, forcing it to return to base.

Bogle

Hags

THE HAG IS AN ARCHETYPAL FIGURE WHO CROPS UP IN MYTH AND
LEGEND AROUND THE WORLD, USUALLY AS A MALEVOLENT FEMALE
SPIRIT IN THE FORM OF A WIZENED OLD WOMAN. MANY STORIES LINK
THE HAG WITH NIGHTMARES; SHE SITS ON THE SLEEPER'S CHEST AND
CAUSES TERRIFYING DREAMS. WHEN THE SLEEPER AWAKENS, HE MAY
FEEL AS IF HE CANNOT BREATHE FOR A SHORT PERIOD. IN ANCIENT
LORE, THIS STATE WAS CALLED BEING "HAG-RIDDEN," THOUGH THE
SENSATION IS EXPLAINED TODAY AS A NATURAL SYNDROME CALLED
"SLEEP PARALYSIS."

Celtic and Norse Hags

The Norse Hag is called a Mara or Mare. She enters a person's bedroom through the keyhole or the door to "ride" the sleeper and bring nightmares. The words for "nightmare" in several European languages derive from this belief, such as the Swedish *mardröm* ("mare dream") and the Norwegian *mareritt* ("mare rid"). Women could become Maras, either by wicked actions or by being cursed.

A related creature from Polish mythology is called the Nocnitsa (Night Hag). Her speciality is tormenting sleeping children. To protect their children, Polish mothers would place an iron knife in their cradles or draw a protection circle around the cradle with a knife.

Another kind of Hag appears in the folklore of Ireland and Scotland. Called the Cailleach, she is a huge, hideous old woman, often carrying a staff, who is associated with the destructive powers of nature. In Scotland, her face is blue and she wears a plaid. She comes down from her mountain home on Samhain (November 1) beating her staff against the ground, which causes it to freeze and brings on cold winds

and snowstorms. Various mountains, rock cairns, and other geographical features are said to have been created by rocks dropped from her apron as she wanders the land.

In Irish myth, the Cailleach keeps the "Summer Maiden" captive until she is rescued by one of the Hag's compassionate sons and warm weather can return.

Gorgon

In Greek mythology, the Gorgones are three monstrous female creatures or Hags, the most famous of whom is Medusa. Ancient Greek vase paintings depict the three sisters as winged women, with broad round heads, large staring eyes, gaping mouths, protruding tongues, the tusks of swine, and living snakes as hair. Legend says that blood taken from the right side of a Gorgon could bring a corpse back to life, yet blood taken from her left side was an instantly fatal poison.

Medusa, the only Gorgon who is mortal, was originally a beautiful woman. According to Ovid, she had many human

Medusa

on her breastplate to strike dread in her foes. By tradition, everyone who laid eyes upon Medusa's awful face was turned to stone. In another myth, Hercules used a lock of Medusa's hair to protect a town from attack. These tales are remembered in the practice of placing a carved stone Gorgon head above doors and on walls, coins, shields, and tombstones in hopes of warding off evil influences.

Symbol of female power

Some scholars have argued that rather than being a monster, the terrifying Gorgon is a holy image of female power and wisdom. Her wide unblinking eyes symbolize the ability to penetrate illusions and see the truth. Her boar tusks come from the sacred pigs, an archaic symbol of rebirth, which were sacrificed to Athena in ancient Athens. Her serpentine hair is a reminder of the cycle of birth, death, and regeneration represented by the snake's shedding and renewing its skin. Seen in this way, the purpose of the terrifying Gorgon mask was to guard and protect women and the mysteries of the Divine Feminine.

suitors but also attracted the attentions of Poseidon, the god of the sea. One day the god found her alone and ravished her in a temple sacred to the virgin goddess Athena. Outraged at this desecration, Athena transformed Medusa's lovely hair to loathsome snakes, then she placed the fearful face of the monster she had created

Baba Yaga

The Hag of Russian and eastern European folklore is Baba Yaga. Like other Hags, she is a wizened old woman with a long hooked nose. Like Medusa, she is fearsome and hideous, with bulging eyes that petrify anyone she looks upon.

Baba Yaga lives in a hut in a birch forest that constantly whirls around on chicken legs. The hut's windows shut like eyes and its keyhole has sharp teeth. Surrounding the hut is a fence made of human bones and decorated with skulls. Each day, three ghostly riders visit the hut, one dressed in white, one in red, and one in black. Baba Yaga herself travels through the air in a mortar, which she rows with its pestle. As she flies, she sweeps the air with her birch broom to clean her tracks behind her.

In fairy tales, Baba Yaga is portrayed as a cannibalistic witch who lures human victims, especially children, to her hut and devours them. In the Russian fairy tale "Vasilissa the Beautiful," a young girl is sent by her wicked stepmother to fetch fire from Baba Yaga's hut. Baba Yaga sets a series of tasks the girl must perform on pain of death. With the help of a magical doll she had been given by her mother, Vasilissa performs the tasks perfectly and is reunited with her loving father.

Female nature spirit

Though stories present her as witch-like, scholars believe that Baba Yaga was originally a potent female nature spirit, a provider of healing, protection, and guidance. Connected like Medusa to the cycle of life and death, in early tales she is the Keeper of the Waters of Life and Death. She drops a bit of each kind of water on a victim, which allows the body to die and the soul to be reborn. Her ancient link to the cycles of nature is echoed by the three ghostly riders, who represent day (white), the noon sun (red), and night (black).

Baba Yaga

PART FOUR

Nature spirits

Between the shadow and the sacred

NATURE SPIRITS HOLD A PLACE IN THE HUMAN IMAGINATION HALFWAY
BETWEEN THE MALEVOLENT CREATURES OF THE SHADOW WORLD AND
THE SACRED CREATURES OF WORLD MYTH. ONE THEORY ABOUT THE
ORIGIN OF FAIRIES HOLDS THAT THEY ARE "DEMOTED ANGELS"—
FORMERLY DIVINE BEINGS CAUGHT BETWEEN HEAVEN AND HELL,
WHOSE CHARACTER IS A COMBINATION OF BENEFICENCE AND CRUELTY.

This section begins by tracing nature spirits back to their mythological origins. The semi-divine figures of Pan in Greek myth and the Green Man in Celtic and European myth are representations of the spirit of wild nature itself. The Greek Nymphs and the Hindu Devas are defenders and controllers of aspects of nature, including the forests, rivers, mountains, heavenly bodies, winds, and clouds. Growing out of these myths, are the elementals—spirits who embody the energy of the four natural elements: air, earth, fire, and water.

Closely linked to nature spirits are the "little people" known in various cultures as Fairies, Elves, and Dwarves. It is often hard to draw clear distinctions between these creatures. For instance, the dark Elves of Norse myth, the

Green Man

housekee
appear at
their da ly w

Most of the
are mischievou
rather than acti
them are willin
leave them foo

But people w
them or who
and its creat
wrath. The V
Europe, ma
animals into
them to d
creatures know
breath as a fog
come too close

Faunus

eece, Pan was the spirit of wild
the protector of woodlands,
ins, hunting, and shepherds and
. Classical images depict him as a
ie horns, legs and tail of a goat,
and pointed ears. He is often
ig the pelt of a lynx. In Roman
being similar in appearance to
Faunus and serves many of the
ns as Pan.

n the Olympian gods, "Pan"
the Greek word *paon*, which
man." Because he was said to
to experience sudden fear in
lonely places, his name is also the origin of
the word "panic."

Lusty and wild, Pan delighted in playing
rustic music on his flute. The story of his
first set of pipes is told in Ovid's
Metamorphoses. Syrinx was a beautiful
Nymph who was pursued by many suitors,
all of whom she rejected. One day, as she
was returning from a hunt, she met Pan,
who instantly desired her. With Pan in hot
pursuit, Syrinx ran to the banks of the River
Ladon and called to the river Nymphs to
save her. Just as Pan reached out to grab
her, the Nymphs pulled Syrinx under
the water and she was transformed into
river reeds. In her honor, Pan plucked
the hollow reeds and fashioned them
into a set of pipes on which he played a
country melody.

Roman Faunus

Faunus often wears a wolfskin and carries a
goblet. Honored as a fertility spirit, he
was also a guardian of wild nature and
agricultural herds. Because he protected
cattle from attacks by wolves, Faunus was
also called Lupercus ("he who wards off the
wolf"). Each February 15, a festival in his
honor called the Lupercalia was celebrated
in Rome. Priests dressed in goatskins
walked through the streets hitting
spectators with belts made of goat's hide.
The festival was aimed at assuring the
fruitfulness of the land and the increase
of flocks.

Pan

Nymph

In Greek mythology, Nymphs are female spirits associated with particular places or functions in nature. Often they serve in the retinue of one of the Olympian gods, especially Artemis, goddess of the hunt.

In appearance, Nymphs are young, beautiful, gentle girls. Though they are long-lived, they are not immortal, and their lives end with the death of the particular natural object, such as a tree, to which they are attached. Often worshipped in grottoes and natural shrines, Nymphs personify the fertile and creative powers of nature, such as the life-giving flow of fresh-water springs.

Various aspects of nature have their own particular kind of Nymph:

- **Water Nymphs**, called Nereids, are similar to Mermaids. The 3,000 Oceanids, the Nymphs of the oceans, are the daughters of the Titans Oceanus and Tethys (see pages 128–129).
- **Land Nymphs** are linked to particular geographic locations. Oreids, who inhabit mountains and ravines, often accompany Artemis on hunting expeditions. Alseids protect glens and groves, while Auloniads are found in pastures and mountain valleys, often in the retinue of Pan.
- **Wood Nymphs** are identified with particular species of trees. Often their bodies become part of the trees they inhabit. Dryads are associated with oak trees, Hamadryads with nut, elm, and fig trees, and Meliae with ash trees.

Ovid tells the story of Daphne, the Nymph who becomes a laurel tree. The god of love Eros wounds Apollo the god of the Sun, with an arrow, causing him to fall in love with Daphne, daughter of the river god Peneus. A follower of Artemis and vowed to chastity, Daphne runs away from her pursuer. Just as Apollo is about to catch her, Daphne cries out to her father for help. The moment the cry leaves her lips, her skin turns to bark, her hair to leaves, her arms to branches and her feet to roots. Embracing the lovely laurel tree, Apollo declares it sacred and winds a laurel wreath around his brow.

Wood Nymph

Lares

Ancient Romans honored mythical beings that served as guardian spirits of a particular place, such as a forest, hill, river, or crossroads. These beings, called *Lares* or *genii loci*, did not move around freely; they stayed within the boundaries of the place that they protected.

Most artworks depicting Lares show them in the form of dancing youths with a horn cup in one hand and a bowl in the other, often accompanied by a snake. A shrine to such spirits, called a *lararium*, was a feature in every Roman home. The shrine looked like a small cupboard in which the Lares were housed in the form of tiny statuettes. Often the *lararium* also housed an image of a snake, an ancient symbol of the generative power of the head of the household. Prayers for protection and offerings of special foods were made daily at the shrine so that the lares would bless the household and bring fertility to its fields.

Huldra

In Scandinavian folklore, the Huldra is a wood Nymph who guards the forests and the flocks. She spends her days caring for the flocks and singing on the mountainsides.

From the front, the Huldra looks like a beautiful young woman with long hair. In some depictions she is naked; in others, she is dressed as a dairymaid. But from behind, the Huldra is hollow, like the trunk of a tree, and she often has a long tail like a cow or a fox that she tries to conceal.

Some stories tell of marriages between Huldra women and human men. In one tale, a Huldra beats a man who had promised, and failed, to keep their engagement secret with her cow's tail until he loses his hearing and his wits. In another, she reminds a husband who is treating her badly of her magical powers by straightening out a horseshoe still glowing from the forge with her bare hands.

Lares

Cernunnos

Cernunnos

Lord of the Animals in Celtic mythology, Cernunnos is the protector of wild animals. He is thought to be related to Pan (see page 241) and to the Minotaur (see page 81), as well as having some similarities with the Hindu Lord of the Animals Pashupati.

On the 1st-century BCE Gundestrup Cauldron, a silver vessel found in Denmark, Cernunnos is depicted as a man seated in a cross-legged posture, wearing a tight-fitting, striped shirt and trousers. On his head are deer antlers. Around his neck is a royal torc or ring. In one hand, he holds another torc; in the other he holds a serpent with the horns of a ram. The figure is surrounded by animals including a stag, a wild pig, and a wolf.

Images of Cernunnos likely had ceremonial and religious significance linked to wild nature and the fertility of the herds and fields. As the Lord of the Hunt, he punishes those who needlessly injure the animals under his protection. Similar images, such as the stag-headed figure painted in a Paleolithic cave at Trois-Frères, France, date back to around 13,000 BCE.

The Green Man

The Green Man is a spirit from the folklore of ancient Europe. He is a symbol of the rebirth, fertility and regeneration that takes place in the natural world.

He is usually depicted as a head or face surrounded by or composed of foliage, with oak leaves and branches entwined in his hair and beard or issuing from his mouth. Stone carvings of the Green Man can be seen as decorations in medieval churches and cathedrals from as early as the 6th century.

The Green Man represents the spirit of the green world and the life force of trees, plants, and foliage.

In the 16th and 17th centuries, May Day celebrations in English villages often featured a greenery-clad male figure similar to the Green Man called Green George or Jack in the Green. In observances reminiscent of pagan fertility rites, the man wearing the greenery or an effigy of him was dunked into a pond or river to ensure that there would be enough rainfall to make the meadows and pastures green.

Apsaras and Gandharva

An Asparsas (plural apsarases) is a female spirit of the clouds and waters in Hindu-Buddhist mythology. The Apsarases are servants of Indra, king of the demi-gods. The Gandharvas are male spirits with great musical skills and delight in playing music so that the Apsarases can dance.

In appearance, Apsarases are beautiful young women dressed in elegant silks and wearing elaborate headdresses. Skilled dancers, they often entertain at the courts of the gods, dancing to the music produced by their husbands, the Gandharvas, who are sometimes depicted as being part-bird or part-horse.

Apsarases appear in many episodes in Hindu epics such as the *Mahabharata*. In one typical tale, the god Indra sends the Apsaras Menaka to distract the sage Viswamitra from his ascetic practices in order to prevent the sage from gaining enough power to challenge the authority of the gods. At first, the sage ignores Menaka's sensuous dance. But then a gust of wind blows away her only garment and the sage succumbs to her charms.

Natural Devas

In Hindu mythology, the Devas or "shining ones" are demi-gods, celestial beings that control various forces of nature such as fire, wind, air, thunder, and the sea. In Hindu art, Devas usually appear as heroic or supremely beautiful humans, sometimes with multiple arms or heads or with animal features.

Similar to angels in the Judeo-Christian tradition, Devas play prominent roles in Hindu mythology, especially in their perpetual battles against the asuras or demons (see pages 216–217).

Specific Devas within Hindu mythology are responsible for particular elements of nature:

- **Vayu** is the Deva of the air and winds. Riding an antelope and carrying a white banner, he stirs the clouds and personifies the breath of all breathing beings.
- **Agni** is the Deva of fire. He has seven tongues of fire and sharp golden teeth. Riding a ram, he carries offerings burned in his fire to the supreme gods. His two heads symbolize his dual nature as heavenly light and destructive earthly fire.

Sculpture of dancing Apsarases.

- **Ushas** is the Devi (female Deva) of dawn. An attractive and beautifully adorned young woman, she rides in the chariot of Surya, Deva of the Sun. She brings illumination, awakening, and growth to living beings.

- **Chandra** is the Deva of the Moon. He drives the Moon chariot across the sky, pulled by ten white horses. He causes dew to fall on plants, giving them life. Prayers to Chandra can help a couple conceive a child.

Elementals

IN THE 16TH CENTURY, A SWISS ALCHEMIST, PHYSICIAN, AND NATURAL
PHILOSOPHER WHO CALLED HIMSELF PARACELSUS (1493–1541) DEVISED
A THEORY AIMED AT LINKING THE NATURE SPIRITS OF THE GREEKS AND
ROMANS TO HIS OWN MEDICAL, CHRISTIAN, AND OCCULT BELIEFS.

Gnome

The four elements

Paracelsus argued that the "dem
believed to cause mental illnesses
"natural" rather than "supernatural"
Halfway between flesh and spir
beings were able to eat, ta
and reproduce like human b
spirits, however, they were a
their shape and move throug
great rapidity.

Paracelsus divided these b
elementals, into four gre
to the four elements, w
considered the fundament
of nature since the time

• Air elementals or Sylph the air around an
• Earth elementals or or her with their
• Fire elementals or S g of the beauty and
• Water elementals o

Gnome

Earth elementals, according to Paracelsus, are the Gnomes that dwell in caverns and other subterranean places. They are grotesque little creatures about 12–18 in. (30–45 cm) tall. Most look like little old men, with long white beards and rotund bellies, and are usually dressed in green or russet brown.

Because the earth is their native element, Gnomes easily scamper out of holes in the stumps of trees and can vanish by dissolving into a tree or into the ground. Some Gnome communities live in vast underground palaces that are constructed of alabaster and marble, ruled over by their king, whose name is Gob.

Gnomes are guardians of earthly treasures, including minerals, metals, and precious stones. Their work includes cutting crystals into rocks and developing veins of ore. Authorities disagree about their disposition. Some say that Gnomes are friendly and helpful to humankind. Paracelsus, however, cautioned that Gnomes can be malicious or tricky until a person wins their trust.

Gnome

Salamander

The elemental of fire was the Salamander, according to Paracelsus, who described the creature as thin, red, and dry-skinned—like a wisp of flame—and having a wrathful disposition. Other authorities, including Pliny the Elder, described Salamanders as looking like lizards with scaly skin and about 12 in. (30 cm) long.

In medieval belief, Salamanders were essential for fire to exist; without them, it was impossible for a match, flint, or steel to give off a spark. Renaissance artist and scientist Leonardo da Vinci wrote that Salamanders ate fire.

The link between Salamanders and fire is very ancient. A passage in the Jewish Talmud (c. 200–500 CE) says that the Salamander is produced fire and that anyone smeared with its blo is immune to being burned. This belief have arisen because the real-life lizard c a Salamander would crawl out from a p of wood in which it had been hibernati when the log was burned.

Salamander

mothers feared that Fairies might steal their babies and substitute a Fairy child, called a changeling, or an enchanted piece of wood for the stolen baby. Adults could also be abducted and taken into the "hollow hills"— often, ancient burial mounds —where the Fairies were said to live. Eating Fairy food would prevent the person from ever returning to the human realm.

Among the most fascinating compilations of fairy lore is *The Secret Commonwealth* written by Scottish clergyman Robert Kirk in 1691, shortly before his mysterious death. According to legend, Kirk was walking on a Fairy hill near his church in Aberfoyle when he fell into a swoon and was taken for dead. He later appeared to a relative in a dream saying that he had been abducted to Fairyland, where he remains captive to this day.

Fairy

Fairy classification

Fairies have been classified in a number of ways, depending on the mythology and culture. Two of the most useful divisions divide Fairies into the Seelie Court and the Unseelie Court.

The Seelie Court

In Scottish folklore, the Seelie (meaning "blessed" or "holy") Court is the community of helpful and beneficent Fairies. Often seen at twilight in long, solemn processions, these Fairies are willing to seek help from humans and to return human kindness with gifts and favors. For instance, they often leave gifts of corn and bread for poor country folk who honor them. They enjoy feasting, hunting, and dancing.

The Unseelie Court

This particular classification of Fairies is malicious towards humankind. At night, they may appear in a group or "horde" to harass travelers by taking them up into the air, pinching them, tangling their hair into knots, or leading them astray. These creatures are also believed to be responsible for sickness and death among domestic animals. They prefer to live in the wilderness and in places associated with

The Fairy Ride

bloodshed, such as burial grounds and ancient battlefields.

Trooping Fairies and solitary Fairies

Celtic folklorists such as Irish poet William Butler Yeats (1865–1939) distinguish between Fairies who live in communities and Fairies who live alone. Trooping Fairies prefer to wear green and range from creatures tiny enough to wear caps made of flower bells to those large enough to communicate with humans. Some trooping Fairies are friendly towards humans while others are sinister. Mortals can eavesdrop on the society of trooping Fairies by entering a Fairy mound, though doing so can be deadly.

Solitary Fairies are often associated with a specific household, place, or occupation. They prefer to wear red, brown, or gray rather than green. They disdain the Fairy dances and gay amusements of the trooping Fairies, often preferring to interact with humans. For instance, solitary Fairies may offer gifts and wishes to humans they encounter, though the consequences of accepting a Fairy gift are unpredictable.

Sidhe

The Sidhe (pronounced shee) are the trooping Fairies of Ireland and Highland Scotland. The name comes from the ancient burial mounds called *sidhe* under which they are said to live. The aristocrats of the Fairy world, the Sidhe are tall and stunningly beautiful, with soft skin and long flowing hair. They are renowned for their great age and great power.

According to tradition, the Sidhe are the remnants of the gods and deified heroes of Celtic mythology, including the Tuatha De Danann (people of the goddess Danu), who agreed to dwell in the Otherworld after their defeat by the Milesians (a Celtic people who migrated to Ireland) in Celtic prehistory. At festival times, such as Midsummer and Samhain, they come into this world for dances and revelry. In folk belief and practice, traditional people leave offerings for the Sidhe and take care not to anger them or even to name them directly, calling them instead "the Fair Folk" or the "People of Peace."

Morgan le Fay

A powerful Fairy queen and priestess of magic in the legends surrounding King Arthur, stately and beautiful Morgan le Fay (Morgan the fairy) presided over a sisterhood of nine who lived on the enchanted island of Avalon (the Isle of Apples).

In early Arthurian legends, Morgan is a benevolent Fairy who aids Arthur throughout his life. In later tales, she becomes Arthur's half-sister and the mother of Mordred, the son born of an incestuous union with her brother. It is Mordred who mortally wounds Arthur in his final battle and who takes the wounded king to his place of healing in Avalon.

The process of Morgan's demotion from a powerful goddess to a sinister enchantress and seductress parallels the denigration of the Fairy host by medieval Christian writers. Like other women healers and miracle workers of the Middle Ages, Morgan was vilified as a witch and sorceress by Christian chroniclers who feared natural magic and feminine wisdom.

Sidhe

Fairies of Midsummer Night

Though it reflects the folk beliefs of its day, the portrayal of the Fairy kingdom in William Shakespeare's *A Midsummer Night's Dream* draws a portrait of the Fairy world that has altered popular conceptions for all time. The play is set in the Athens of Greek mythology, but the trooping Fairies who haunt the woods on the Midsummer Night of the play's action are entirely British.

Oberon, the darkly majestic Fairy king, has been quarreling with his consort Titania, the lovely Fairy queen, over a changeling boy that Titania adopted because the child's mother, dead in childbirth, was a devotee in her cult. Oberon wants the child to join his Fairy troop, but Titania has refused. Their quarrel has disrupted wild nature, causing fogs and tempests.

To punish Titania, Oberon orders his follower Puck—also known as Robin Goodfellow—to sprinkle the juice of a magical flower in Titania's eyes. The juice causes her to fall in love with the first person she sees when she awakes, which turns out to be a comical Athenian workman whose human head has been magically replaced with that of an ass. This same love juice, sprinkled in the eyes of ill-matched human lovers, drives the play's romantic plot.

The dances and woodland revels of the Fairy troops would have been deeply familiar to Shakespeare's audience, as would the links between Fairies and changelings, wild nature and magic. Moreover, the character of Puck as a mischievous nature spirit, also called a Brownie or Hobgoblin, who delights in country pranks like frightening milkmaids and spooking horses was well known in Shakespeare's day. However, Shakespeare's Fairies are more concerned with human affairs and more beneficent than the traditional conception. Their intervention in the unhappy love affairs of the human characters and their blessing of the marriages with which the play ends humanizes the Fairy world and makes it for all time more friendly, charming and accessible.

Fairies of *A Midsummer Night's Dream*.

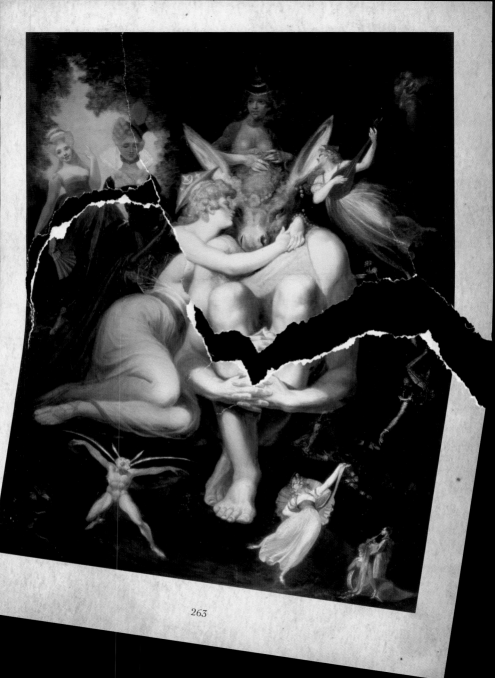

Vila

The Fairies of eastern Europe, the Vila, are often depicted as beautiful winged women, naked or dressed in white with long flowing hair, although they are shape-shifters and can also appear as swans, horses, snakes, or falcons, or as natural phenomena such as whirlwinds. The Vila live deep in the forest. They are fierce protectors of its animals and plants and are revered for their deep knowledge of herbal healing. Humans who harm _____ may be lured into a mag____ ___ _ death, crushed ___ ____ ____ their creatures ___ __gic circle and danced t___ in a landslide or drowned in a river.

Various stories are told about the or___ of the Vila. Some say that they are the spir__ of women who are caught between __ world and the afterlife because of the frivolous habits. A more romant__ explanation is that they are the spirits _ betrothed gir__ ___ __ore their wedding ni__ts who died be___ in their gr__ and are unable to rest __t quietly ___es.

Vila

Peri

Ancient Persia was the home of a group of Fairies known as Peri. These tiny, winged female nature spirits were so beautiful that they shimmered with all the colors of the rainbow.

Before the coming of Islam, Peris were held responsible for catastrophic natural events such as comets, eclipses of the Sun and crop failures. With the advent of Islam, the Peris were deemed to be fallen angels, who repented of their transgressions too late to be restored to Heaven. Tales are told of how the Prophet Muhammad was sent to convert them to Islam.

In the earlier Zoroastrian faith of Persia, the Peris are thought to represent the light and good forces of nature that are constantly at war with the dark and evil forces called Deevs. Tales tell of the Deevs capturing Peris and locking them in iron cages at the top of trees, where they are sustained by eating the odor of perfumes brought to them by other Peris.

Peri

Elves

...S IS DIVIDED INTO TWO STRANDS. IN
...APED CREATURES, WHO GENERALLY
...INTED CAPS. THEY EMPLOY THEIR
...RE WONDERFUL THINGS, FROM
...ANTA'S NORTH POLE WORKSHOP.
...M THEIR DEPICTION IN J.R.R.
...TRILOGY, THEY ARE SEEN AS
...O BEINGS, MORE BEAUTIFUL AND
...AND ETERNALLY YOUTHFUL,
...RABLE POWERS TO BATTLE THE
...ELVES ARE A UNIQUE LITERARY
...TS OF TRADITIONAL FOLKLORE
...HERN EUROPE.

...enevolent towards humankind, much like ...ngels. Heroes could become Light Elves ...fter death, and marriages between Light ...ves and human women were also possible. The offspring of such unions were said to be more beautiful than ordinary humans due to their elven blood.

...e
...cording to
...s. They inhabit
...d Alfheim, located
...d Earth, and are always

The Dark Elves or *Döckalfar* are described in the *Eddas* as being unlike the Light Elves in appearance and in actions.

and weave them into a wreath. Passing children through this wreath three times was thought to protect them from Elves.

Spae-wives

The female Elves of Icelandic folklore are the Spae-wives. They look like tiny peasant women, as small as a human finger. They make their homes in the long barrows and sacred mounds of ancient burial places and are experts in magical healing and herbal lore. Gifted in divination—the word *spae* means "prophecy" in Old Norse—Spae-wives can foretell the future by reading tea leaves, runes, and natural omens.

Elle Folk

Known as Elle Folk, in Denmark, Elf women are human-sized with long blond ~tirely hollow back. They enjoy *he lyre, which they do hunters are often harms. Elle men are shorter than the women. They look like little old bearded men wearing dark, close-fitting hats. The Elle Folk live in Ellemounds on the country's windswept moors. They are dangerous to humankind because they can blow their breath as a fog of sickness over any person who comes too close to their dwellings.

Duendes

The house Elves of Spanish folklore are known as Duendes. Female Duendes look like small, middle-aged women with long fingers, dressed in green, red, or gray. Male Duendes wear brimless, conical hats, dark hoods, or red caps.

At night, Duendes emerge from the whitewashed walls of village houses and spend the hours until dawn cleaning, repairing, or working as smiths. Malicious Duendes also break things, make messes, and bring nightmares to the human family whose house they inhabit.

Brownie

Brownie

Similar to Elves, Brownies are the helpful household spirits of English and Scottish folklore. In appearance, Brownies are like small humans, with wrinkled faces and short, brown curly hair. They are usually dressed in brown clothing including a conical hat or hood.

Most Brownies are attached to a single household or farm, where they may reside for centuries. They are protective of their homes and become upset when humans quarrel or do not treat their animals with kindness.

Industrious but shy, Brownies come out at night to do their work, which might include cleaning the house or barn, grinding grain, or churning butter. To repay Brownies for their help, householders leave them a bowl of cream or porridge or a freshly baked loaf of bread. Because Brownies are easily insulted, it is important never to criticize their work. Once offended, a Brownie is likely to undo everything he has done and to abandon the household.

Kobald

The household spirit of German folklore is the Kobald. Like a Brownie, a Kobald looks like a little old man with a wizened face. His name comes from *kobe*, which means "house" and *hode*, which means "beautiful" or "good."

Having a Kobald living near the hearth or in the barn or stables helps to makes any house beautiful. As long as he has been left his share of supper, a Kobald will complete any household task that has been left unfinished while the family sleeps.

A legend tells of the Kobalds of the city of Cologne who did so much work at night that the city's citizens could be lazy all day. Once, a tailor's wife got so curious to see the Kobalds at work that she scattered peas on to the floor of the workshop to make them slip and fall. Infuriated, the Kobalds disappeared, leaving the people of Cologne to do all the work themselves without magical help.

Kobald

271

Dwarf

Dwarves or "little people" who look like stocky old men with oddly shaped noses and feet are found in folklore all over the world. In most versions, they are creatures of the earth who prefer to live in mountain caves or underground mines.

Like the Dark Elves of Norse mythology, Dwarves are expert at fashioning metal into magical objects, including swords, helmets, shields, coats of mail, and rings. Often they are shape-shifters and in some tales, they possess a magical object such as a cloak or ring that makes them invisible.

The Dwarves of Germanic myth can be divided into three groups: White Dwarves are gentle and peaceful and spend their winters underground creating beautiful gold and silver objects, but in the summer, they frolic in the meadows and woodlands. Brown Dwarves are similar in appearance to Brownies, but they are more dangerous. They have been known to steal human babies, play tricks on their chosen household and bring people bad dreams.

Black Dwarves are entirely malicious. They create false lights to lure ships on to the rocks so that they can plunder the cargo; they also use their metalworking skill to create deadly weapons that they strengthen with magical curses.

North American Dwarves

Dwarves also occur in Native American mythology: the Red Dwarf (*Nain Rouge*) of Detroit, Michigan, is considered to be an omen of disaster. The small creature with blazing red eyes is said to have appeared in 1701 to Antoine de la Mothe Cadillac, the city's first white settler. Soon after, Cadillac lost his fortune and was recalled to France. In 1763, the creature appeared to herald Pontiac's rebellion, an uprising of Native American tribes against the British. The Dwarf appeared again in 1805, just before the city burned to the ground. According to urban legend, in 1967 the Nain Rouge was spotted doing cartwheels down the center of a Detroit street on the night a police raid sparked a riot.

White Dwarf

Piskie

These "little people"—sometimes called Piskies or Pixies—from the folklore of the British counties of Devon and Cornwall are wingless and human-shaped, with eyes that slant upward, pointed ears, and often wear pointed hats.

Though they sometimes help families with their chores when they are treated with respect and left bowls of food or saucers of milk, in most stories, they are mischievous. Piskies enjoy playing tricks on unsuspecting humans, like leading them astray on the moors or stealing their horses and returning them with tangled manes.

Piskies have also been known to "borrow" human children. A little boy from St. Allen, Cornwall, was missing for three days. When he was found asleep, exactly where his mother had last seen him, he told of having been taken to a cave sparkling with jewels, where he was fed honey and sung to sleep by beings that looked like stars in a night sky.

Piskie

274

Leprechaun

One of the "little people" of Irish folklore, Leprechauns are tricky Dwarf-like creatures who take the form of little old men dressed in green with silver buckles on their shoes and a high-crowned hat. By trade, Leprechauns are cobblers and are sometimes depicted wearing a leather apron and tapping away with a hammer on a single shoe.

Reputed to be very wealthy, Leprechauns have buried crocks of gold and treasure. Though a Leprechaun cannot escape if someone keeps an eye fixed on him, if the person looks away for even a second, the Leprechaun will vanish laughing. A typical tale tells of a man who forces a Leprechaun to reveal the bush under which a pot of gold is buried. The man marks the bush with a red garter and goes off to fetch a spade to dig up the treasure. When he returns, he finds that every bush in the field is decorated with an identical red garter!

Leprechaun

PART FIVE

Sacred creatures

Heroes, gods, and religious beings

ALL OF THE WORLD'S SACRED TRADITIONS TELL STORIES ABOUT THEIR
GODS AND HEROES. SOME PEOPLE CONSIDER THESE STORIES TO BE THE
LITERAL TRUTH, ESPECIALLY THOSE TOLD WITHIN THEIR OWN TRADITION,
WHILE OTHERS BELIEVE THESE NARRATIVES TO BE A PRODUCT OF THE
IMAGINATION. IN BOTH CASES, SACRED MYTHS EMBODY A HIGHER
TRUTH, ONE THAT IS PROFOUND AND UNIVERSALLY INSPIRING.

The sacred stories retold in this section are coded with significance—not, perhaps, about the actual events of prehistory, but about the hopes, desires, fears, and potential of human beings the world over. As you read, you may conclude that you have more in common with the people of the past than you thought, since the same issues that moved our ancestors concern us today. Good and evil, subsistence and abundance, children and family, love and death, and the role that the Divine plays in providing for our needs and protecting us from harm are as familiar to us as they would have been to our ancestors thousands of years ago.

Though many of the sacred creatures described in this section are gods and goddesses, the coverage is by no means comprehensive. All of the sacred beings included here are connected in some way to mythic creatures. In some cases, their appearance links them to the fabulous beasts, such as the animal-headed gods and goddesses of ancient Egypt or the Hopi Kachinas of the American southwest. In others, the stories involve animal manifestations or transformations, such as the avatars of the Hindu god Vishnu or the forms taken by the Greek god Zeus in his amorous adventures. Other stories told here are the hero cycles in which a semi-divine figure battles a series of opponents, including many mythic creatures; the Labors of Hercules are one example.

In every case, these myths arise from the ability that most distinguishes human beings from other creatures: we are storytellers, the ones who tell the tales about all of the other creatures—including, as you will discover, the gods.

Ryujin

Myths of the ancient Middle East

THE FERTILE VALLEYS OF THE TIGRIS AND EUPHRATES RIVERS (NOW
MODERN-DAY IRAQ AND PART OF IRAN) GAVE RISE TO A SERIES OF
ANCIENT CULTURES COLLECTIVELY KNOWN AS MESOPOTAMIA.

Mesopotamian civilizations

The earliest of these civilizations were Sumeria (c.3100–2000 BCE) and Akkadia (c.2350–2200 BCE). Later cultures, such as Babylonia (c.2000–1600 BCE) and Assyria

Marduk

(c.1350–612 BCE), were centered in vast city-states, protected by massive walls and featured monumental temples and palaces. The head of state was a semi-divine king whose authority was confirmed in elaborate rituals and sacred festivals.

These great civilizations developed a sophisticated set of religious beliefs and mythical stories, many of which were recorded by temple scribes on clay tablets using the cuneiform scripts developed by the Sumerians and Akkadians. The discovery in the mid-19th century of these tablets in the royal archives of such cities as Ur, Babylon, and Nineveh and their subsequent decipherment by scholars revealed to the modern world the exploits of mythical gods and semi-divine kings such as Marduk and Gilgamesh, including their epic battles with fabulous and monstrous creatures.

Cylinder seal showing the bird-man Zu and the water god Ea.

Mesopotamia's mythical creatures

In addition to tablet texts, the heroes and creatures of Mesopotamia are preserved in works of art, ranging from monumental sculptures to delicately inscribed cylinder seals. These seals—cylinders made of stone, glass, or gemstones such as lapis lazuli—were engraved with picture stories and were used to roll an impression on to a soft clay surface. A seal depicting the slaying of the monstrous Humbaba by Gilgamesh and his companion Enkidu is displayed in the British Museum in London. So influential was Mesopotamian culture that surrounding civilizations, including Syria-Palestine, Asia Minor (modern-day Turkey), and Persia, incorporated many of its myths and beliefs into their cultures and religions. Some also found their way into the Old and New Testaments of the Bible. Mesopotamian culture came to an end when the region was conquered first by the Persian Empire in 539 BCE and then in 331 BCE by Alexander the Great.

Marduk defeats Tiamat.

Marduk and Tiamat

One of the earliest creation stories is told in the Mesopotamian epic the *Enuma Elish* (c.18th–12th centuries BCE). Recited each spring at the New Year Festival in the great city of Babylon, the myth tells of the battle between Marduk, the chief god of the city, and Tiamat, a Dragon-like monster who stands for the primeval chaos that must be defeated before the Universe can be created and human civilization can flourish.

In the beginning, the myth says, that nothing existed except for two vast oceans—Apsu, the sweet-water ocean and Tiamat, the salt-water ocean. The union of these vast forces brings forth the gods, including the great gods Anu and Ea, who are the parents of Marduk. In appearance, Marduk is a heroic and kingly human, often depicted as bearded and wearing a high crown.

When conflict breaks out between the younger gods and the primeval deities, Ea kills Apsu.

Seeking revenge, Tiamat assembles a horde of monsters called the Girtablili, which includes the fearsome Scorpion-men—human above the waist and scorpions below, whose heads touch the sky and whose glance is death. The horde is led by Kingu, Tiamat's monstrous son, to whom she gives the Tablet of Destiny—a clay tablet inscribed with cuneiform writing that confers supreme authority as ruler of the Universe. Tiamat is also a terrible monster with a horned head, a scaly, snake-like body, powerful forelegs, and an immense tail.

As the gods' champion, Marduk engages Tiamat in fierce combat. The hero ensnares the monster in a net, shoots arrows down her gullet into her heart, and, finally, crushes her skull with his mace. Then he divides her body in two. One half forms the sky and the other half the Earth. After killing Kingu and seizing the Tablet of Destiny, Marduk mixes the blood of Kingu with earth and fashions humankind. According to tradition, human beings were created to do the work of the world so that the gods could rest.

Gilgamesh and the Humbaba

Gilgamesh was king of the Sumerian city of Uruk on the Euphrates River in about 2700 BCE. Many myths about this king, who is said to have been "two-thirds god and one-third man," were recorded in cuneiform script on stone tablets. The fullest version of this story was found at Nineveh, in the ruins of the library of Ashurbanipal, king of Assyria (ruled 669–633 BCE).

Because the young Gilgamesh was oppressing his people, the gods created the ape-like "wild man" Enkidu to keep him in check. Enkidu, who is covered with hair and lives with the wild beasts, becomes more civilized when a temple prostitute seduces him. At first, Enkidu and Gilgamesh fight furiously, but after Enkidu concedes that Gilgamesh is the superior warrior, the two become friends and set forth on a heroic adventure—a journey to the Cedar Forest to cut down the trees to build a great gate for the city of Uruk.

Guarding the forest is a monstrous Giant called the Humbaba. The monster's vast body is covered with armored plates, and it has the legs of a lion ending in vulture's talons, a bull's horns, and a snake's head at the end of its tail. Though the monster begs for its life, at Enkidu's urging, Gilgamesh slices off its head with his sword.

The gods decide that Enkidu must die for his part in the slaying of the Humbaba. Distraught at his friend's death, Gilgamesh sets out to discover the secret of eternal life. After crossing the Waters of Death, he meets a man who tells him of a plant that can confer immortality that grows at the bottom of the sea. Though Gilgamesh ties stones to his feet and retrieves the plant, it is eaten by a snake before he can use it. For this reason, snakes renew themselves by shedding their skin, while human beings must die.

Humbaba

Lamassu

Lamassu are protective deities in the art and mythology of the ancient Middle East. Hybrid creatures, they combine the body of a bull or lion, symbolizing strength, the wings of an eagle, symbolizing freedom and speed, and the head of a bearded man, symbolizing high intelligence.

As colossal statues found in the ruins of ancient Babylonian and Assyrian cities, Lamassu were positioned as gateway guardians at the entrances to royal palaces such as that found at Nineveh. Images of Lamassu were also carved on to tablets buried under the door threshold. Lamassu sculptures have two aspects—when viewed from the front, they appear to be standing guard; when viewed from the side, they appear to be striding forward.

In Mesopotamian mythology, Lamassu help people fight chaos and evil. Each day, they hold the gates of dawn open so that the Sun god Shamash can rise and also help to support the weight of the Sun disc.

Zu

A massive bird-god in the mythologies of ancient Mesopotamia, Zu (also called Anzu) is sometimes depicted as an eagle with the head of a lion. It is also portrayed as a hybrid creature with the body of an eagle and the torso of a man with a beard.

Zu was the servant of the chief sky god Enlil. While Enlil was bathing, Zu stole the Tablet of Destiny (see page 283)—the authority to rule the Universe—and carried it to its nest in the Sabu Mountains. In some versions of the myth, Ea persuades the mother goddess Belet-Ili to give birth to the divine hero Ninurta, who is sent to retrieve the tablets. After a terrible battle, Ninurta pierces Zu's lung with an arrow, killing it and returns the Tablet to Enlil. In other versions, Lugalbanda, the father of Gilgamesh, or Marduk, the Babylonian hero god, defeat Zu and retrieve the Tablet.

Lamassu

Mithra and the bull

Mithra is the Persian (old Iranian) god of light. He helped to maintain the order of the Cosmos and participated in the gods' struggles against evil. Worshipped in secret cults open only to men that began in Persia and Asia Minor and attained their greatest popularity during the Roman Empire, Mithra was believed to protect his followers after death so that their souls were not lost to the forces of darkness. In Roman times, followers of Mithra included men from all walks of life, from emperors to slaves.

Because Mithra was born from a rock in a cave, his temples were often small subterranean chambers, the ceiling painted to look like a starry sky. Each temple featured an image of Mithra killing a sacred bull. Each spring, according to myth, Mithra kills the bull so that its blood can bring forth vines, its spinal cord wheat and its sperm all types of useful animals. According to belief, if humankind is threatened with a disastrous lack of sustenance, Mithra will return from the heavens to kill another divine bull and bring forth a bountiful harvest.

In temple artworks, Mithra wears a short cloak lined with stars and a Phrygian cap—a soft, red conical hat with the top pulled forward, which symbolizes freedom. The sacred bull, which stands for Taurus and symbolizes the spring, is surrounded by other astrological animals: a dog symbolizing the constellations Canus Major or Minor; a serpent symbolizing the constellation Hydra, which drinks the blood of the bull from a wound; a scorpion, which stands for Scorpio and symbolizes the autumn, attacks the bull's testicles, robbing it of strength; and above Mithra are symbols for the Sun and Moon.

In the Mithraic calendar, the holiest day of the week was Sunday and the holiest day of the year was December 25. Religious scholars believe that these and other Mithraic cult beliefs were incorporated into Christianity.

Mithra slays the bull.

Creatures of the Bible

THE BIBLE MENTIONS MORE THAN 120 TYPES OF CREATURE. MOST ARE
ORDINARY ANIMALS, GENERALLY CHARACTERIZED BY THEIR MEANS OF
LOCOMOTION: CREATURES THAT "GO UPON FOUR FEET" SUCH AS
CATTLE, OXEN, AND LIONS; CREATURES THAT "SWIM IN THE WATER" SUCH
AS WHALES AND FISH WITH SCALES, AND FINS; CREATURES "THAT FLY"
SUCH AS BIRDS AND LOCUSTS; AND "CREEPING THINGS" SUCH AS LIZARDS.

The Bible also mentions fabulous animals such as the Griffin and Unicorn. In some cases, these creatures may reflect ancient misunderstandings or be old names for real animals. For instance, some scholars believe the Bible's Unicorn is actually an auroch, an extinct type of horned cattle. In others, the creatures are symbolic or visionary, such as the creatures discussed below.

The Serpent of Eden

The Serpent that tempts Adam and Eve in the Garden of Eden likely reflects the Mesopotamian mythological tradition linking snakes to birth, death, and resurrection, based on their ability to renew themselves by shedding their skin.

Other attributes of real snakes, such as their body shape, which links them to human sexuality, and their forked tongue, which suggests deceitful speech, also figure in the Garden of Eden story.

In Genesis, God commands Adam not to eat from the Tree of Knowledge of Good and Evil. The Serpent tempts Eve to eat the apple, telling her that doing so will make her aware like a god. She does so and convinces Adam to eat the apple as well. Though the pair gain wisdom, they are banished from Paradise for disobeying. The Serpent is cursed "to crawl and eat dust."

Later references in the Bible identify the Serpent with Satan as a cunning deceiver. In European artistic representations, such as

Adam and Eve in the Garden of Eden.

Michelangelo's ceiling for the Sistine Chapel, the Serpent is pictured as having the upper body of a woman, emphasizing its seductiveness.

The beasts of Daniel's vision

In the Old Testament Book of Daniel, which is set during the first year of the reign of Belshezzar, king of Babylonia (reign 553–539 BCE), the Hebrew prophet Daniel relates a prophetic vision that came to him in a dream.

In Daniel's dreams four fabulous beasts arise from the sea and various things happen to them as a consequence:

- A lion with eagle's wings has its wings plucked off. It then stands on two feet like a man and is given a man's heart.
- A bear holds three ribs in its teeth. It is told to devour much flesh.
- A leopard with four wings and four heads is given authority to rule.
- A terrible beast with ten horns devours the whole Earth with its great iron teeth.

The four beasts are said to correspond to four kingdoms. The winged lion stands for Babylonia and Assyria where Lamassu guarded temple and palace entrances. The bear represents Persia and the ribs between its teeth are the Persian empire's principal conquests. The fast-moving winged leopard suggests the swift conquest of the region by Alexander the Great; its four heads suggest the division of Alexander's empire into territories. The beast with ten horns probably represents various rulers of the Roman empire, which certainly seemed to "devour the whole Earth."

The Tetramorph of Ezekiel

Another Hebrew prophet with apocalyptic visions was Ezekiel. While in exile in Babylonia (c.550 BCE), he describes a vision of four creatures, each with the body of a man, the faces of a man, a lion, an ox, and an eagle, and two sets of wings, one above their heads and the other covering their bodies.

Danial dreaming of four monsters.

This creature, called a Tetramorph (from the Greek *tetra* meaning "four"), has been interpreted as combining Babylonian astrological symbols (the man is Aquarius, the lion is Leo, the ox is Taurus, and the eagle is Scorpio) with Christian symbolism, in which the Tetramorph anticipates the four Evangelists of the New Testament.

Lilith

A female demon of the night, similar to a Succubus, Lilith flies around killing newborn children and seducing men so that she can give birth to more demons.

Legends about Lilith are very old. In a version of the Gilgamesh epic, the goddess Ishtar (in Sumeria, her name was Inanna) plants a sacred willow tree in her sanctuary, planning to use the wood for a magical throne. But when she tries to cut down the tree, she finds a snake that cannot be charmed at its base, a Zu bird nesting in its branches, and the Maiden of Darkness, Lilith, living in the trunk. When Gilgamesh kills the serpent, Lilith flies away.

Images of Lilith as a beautiful naked woman, holding the ring and rod of power, with wings and the talons of a Zu bird instead of feet may be based on this myth.

In Jewish Talmudic folklore of the fourth century CE, Lilith is said to be Adam's first wife. Seductive and enchanting, she was created by God in response to Adam's request for a mate. However, Lilith refuses to lie submissively beneath Adam as he desires and when he tries to force her, she abandons him. Though God sends three angels to bring her back, Lilith refuses. Instead, she consorts with evil spirits near the Dead Sea, where each day, she gives birth to more than a hundred demons.

A Muslim legend says that she coupled with Satan and gave birth to the demon Djinn. To punish her for her disobedience, God kills some of her children each day.

In revenge, Lilith preys on newborn infants, especially boys. As recently as the 18th century, a common folk practice in Europe involved protecting newborns with an amulet bearing the images of Adam and Eve, the names of the three angels who were sent to bring Lilith back to Adam and the words "barring Lilith" and "protect this child from harm."

Lilith

Sacred animals and gods of ancient Egypt

ANCIENT EGYPT, WHICH FLOURISHED AS AN ADVANCED CIVILIZATION FOR ABOUT 3,000 YEARS, FROM 3200 BCE TO 332 BCE, HAS GIVEN THE WORLD OF MYTHOLOGY A HOST OF MYTHIC CREATURES. MANY OF THESE ARISE FROM EGYPT'S COMPLEX RELIGIOUS BELIEFS AND PRACTICES.

Gods and goddesses

Based on the ruins of great temple cities like Memphis and Thebes, Egypt is often regarded as a land dominated by gods, kings, and priests. Much of what we know about Egypt's gods comes from the practice of covering the walls of temples with divine images and of sealing sacred paintings, artifacts and artworks into the tombs of Egyptian kings.

Few narratives telling the stories of the gods have been preserved, however, and Egypt's great myths often must be reconstructed from fragmentary religious texts, reliefs on temple walls, and the decorations on coffins and other burial goods. For this reason, the stories of the gods and their depictions often exist in many forms, all of which are "correct" depending on the geographical and chronological context.

Animal heads

Many Egyptian gods are sometimes represented in the form of sacred animals or as humans with animal heads, with the animal head representing one of the god's characteristics. Anubis, the god of embalming and mummification, frequently appears with the body of a man and the head of a black jackal, a canine that prowled the desert and mountain areas where tombs were built. Seket, the goddess of childbirth, appears as a frog, known for fertility.

Papyrus found in Tutankhamun's tomb.

Other Egyptian gods appear in multiple forms. Hathor, the great goddess of Upper Egypt, generally appears as a slim woman wearing a headdress topped by a pair of cow horns with a sun disc between them. But she also appears as a woman with a cow's head or as a lioness, a snake, or a hippopotamus. These part-animal forms were seen as expressing Hathor's attributes: sometimes she expresses the motherly tenderness of a cow; other times, the wildness of a lion or the unpredictability of a snake.

The many legends and myths surrounding Isis and Osiris give rise to a host of mythical creatures, some as representations of the gods. The tension between Osiris and his brother Seth also provide a wealth of imagery and mythical creatures.

Isis and Osiris

Two of the most important Egyptian gods are Osiris, god of agriculture and judge of departed souls in the Underworld, and his consort Isis. Twin brother and sister, they are the children of Nut, the sky goddess, and Geb, the Earth god. The pair are said to have fallen in love in their mother's womb.

Osiris generally appears as a mummified man wearing a white, cone-like headdress and holding a pharaoh's crook and flail. Isis is often depicted as a slim woman wearing a headdress in the shape of an empty throne, though she also appears with cow horns and a Sun disc on her headdress, showing that she has assimilated the qualities of the goddess Hathor. Isis is also shown as a woman with spread wings, indicating her magical powers of resurrection.

Many animal transformations occur in the Isis and Osiris myth. Seth, the brother of Isis and Osiris, who represents the forces of chaos, murders Osiris and dismembers his body. In some versions, Seth takes the form of a crocodile or a hippopotamus to attack his brother. In others, he becomes a bull that tramples Osiris or a mosquito that stings him to death. After dismembering Osiris's body, in some versions Seth buries the pieces all over Egypt; subsequently Osiris rises again with the annual crops of wheat and barley. In other versions, Seth throws the body parts into the Nile.

Weeping and lamenting, Isis searches for and retrieves the parts of her beloved husband's body. In some traditions, she embalms and bandages the body, making Osiris the first mummy. In others, she uses her magical powers to resurrect Osiris long enough for her to conceive their son Horus. Isis hovers above Osiris in the form of a sparrow hawk and fans the breath of life into him with her wings. Images of Isis nursing Horus have been seen as anticipating images of the Virgin Mary with the infant Jesus.

Isis

Seth and Horus

When Horus, the son of Osiris and Isis, grows to manhood, he and Seth fight over who should occupy the empty throne of Osiris. In art, Horus is usually depicted as a man with the head of a falcon while Seth is portrayed as a man with an animal head that has a curved snout and erect square-tipped ears like an aardvark. He also appears entirely in animal form, with a body like a greyhound.

In myth, both Seth and Horus are transformed into many other animals in the course of their conflicts. Seth becomes a donkey or an ox that treads the ripened barley on the threshing floor because the grain embodies the life force of his enemy Osiris. As a bull, Seth gathers followers in the hills, but Isis turns herself into a dog with a knife at the end of her tail and pursues him.

Over the 80 years of their conflict, Horus and Seth battle as bears, lions, and snakes. Seth plucks out the left eye of Horus, while Horus tears off Seth's foreleg and testicles. The battle is interrupted at times for councils of the gods, but the gods are divided as to who should win, so the conflict continues.

Hippo showdown

Finally, Seth and Horus take the form of hippopotamuses and submerge themselves in the Nile. Standing on the shore, Isis cannot distinguish which hippo is her son and which is his adversary. She throws a copper harpoon, but strikes Horus. Correcting her mistake, she harpoons Seth, but releases him when he begs for mercy. Enraged, Horus wounds his mother and flees to the desert, where the goddess Hathor restores his sight with the milk of a gazelle.

In the end, the gods appeal to Osiris who issues a judgment from the Underworld in favor of his son Horus and threatens to release a horde of demons if his son is denied the throne. Horus is crowned, while Seth is summoned to live in the heavens where he becomes the god of storms.

Horus

Hathor

The cow-headed goddess Hathor is much older than Isis. Archaeologists have found her image—a woman's face with cow's ears and horns—adorning the funeral pallet of the pre-dynastic Egyptian king Narmer (c.3100 BCE), an indication that worship of Hathor likely stems from an earlier matriarchal culture. Similar images of Hathor appear on the capitals of pillars at her temple at Dendera, where reverence was paid to her sacred cows.

As a Great Mother, Hathor manifests as lover, mother, avenger, and comforter of the dead. She is the mother and the lover of an earlier version of the hawk- or falcon-headed god Horus (called the elder Horus to distinguish him from the son of Isis and Osiris). In later times, she is said to be the wife of the younger Horus and the mother of his son Ihy. In later myths, her characteristics meld with those of Isis. In one story, the younger Horus cuts off the head of his mother Isis and replaces it with the head of a cow.

The ancient connection of the cow to sexuality and fertility has been explained by some scholars as arising from female reproductive anatomy. The roughly triangular cow head and its two horns resemble the shape of the uterus and fallopian tubes. Moreover, the cow's udders and abundant milk production are an obvious reference to maternal nurturing. A statue of 18th-dynasty pharaoh Amenhotep II (reigned c.1453–1419 BCE) found in the temple complex of Deir el-Bahri shows Hathor in cow form with the king standing protected beneath her head and also kneeling to drink from her udder.

In her role as the goddess of joy, singing, music, dancing, and sexual love, Hathor was worshipped with an ancient rattle called the sistrum. At her temple at Dendera, her son Ihy is depicted as a naked boy holding the sacred rattle and personified jubilation.

Hathor

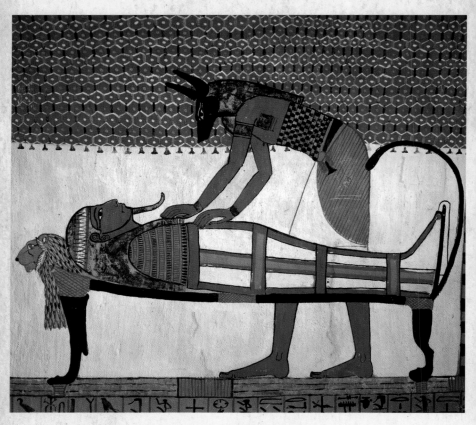

Wall painting showing Anubis bending over the mummy of Sennutem.

Anubis

The son of Osiris and his sister Nepthys, the god Anubis appears with the body of a man and the head of a black jackal. Though jackals prowled around desert tombs, the jackal-like qualities of Anubis are not devouring, but protective, like a watchdog. Prayers to Anubis are carved on the most ancient tombs in Egypt, addressing him as the guardian of the dead.

Skilled in the arts of embalming, Anubis performs the intricate processes of mummification—packing the body with spices, wrapping it in linen, and then casting protective spells that guarantee immortality. In the Egyptian *Book of the Dead*, Anubis leads the deceased soul into the Hall of Judgment, where Osiris presides as Lord of the Underworld. There the heart of the deceased person is weighed on a balance against the feather of the goddess of truth, Ma'at. Those whose hearts are light may journey to a heavenly paradise while those whose hearts are heavy are devoured.

Sobek

The crocodile god Sobek is the son of Neith, sister of Isis. He usually appears as a man with the head of a crocodile holding an ankh—a cross with a handle that is the hieroglyphic character for "life."

Sobek helped the goddess Isis gather the parts of her husband Osiris from the Nile (see also page 298) and he also travels to the Underworld to repair damage done to bodies of the deceased that resulted from the manner of their deaths.

Since crocodiles were common and deeply feared in ancient Egypt, worship of Sobek may have begun as a way of appeasing the crocodiles of the Nile and reducing their threat. The many mummified crocodiles found in tombs demonstrates their importance in Egyptian beliefs. Worship of Sobek was centered in the city of Arsinoe, which the Greeks renamed Crocodopolis. There crocodiles were kept in sacred pools, adorned with jewels and hand-fed meat. In time, Sobek came to be associated with the fertility brought to the land by the annual Nile floods.

Tauret

The hippopotamus fertility goddess Tauret (or Taweret) helps in childbirth, in the daily rebirth of the Sun and in the rebirth of the soul in the Underworld. In appearance, she is a pregnant hippopotamus standing upright, with large human breasts, the hind legs of a lion, and the tail of a crocodile.

In some images, Tauret wears the Sun disc and cow horns like Isis (see pages 298–299), leans on the Sa, a rolled shepherd's shelter symbolizing "protection," and holds the ankh, the hieroglyphic character for "life."

In the birth chamber, she often appears with Bes as a protector and scares away demons that might harm the mother and child. Tauret's connection with birth likely stems from the fact that hippos were common in the fertile mud of the Nile and that hippo mothers were fierce in defending their young. Her image was common on amulets and on milk vessels with a hole in one of her nipples for pouring.

Bes

A dwarf-shaped god who is one of the protectors of the household in Egyptian belief, Bes is fat, bearded, and so ugly that he is almost comical. He is often depicted with a lion's mane, ears, and tail and a plume of feathers on his head. Scholars have noted that his appearance resembles gods found in central Africa, which may indicate his origins.

As a protector of childbirth, Bes dances around the birthing room, shaking his rattle and yelling to frighten away evil spirits. After the baby is born, Bes stays near the cradle to entertain the infant and frighten away bad dreams. When a child laughed for no reason, Bes was said to be nearby making funny faces. Many houses kept a statue of Bes near the doorway to protect the household and its inhabitants from harm. In Dendera, Bes was a companion of Hathor, where he danced, played the lyre and tambourine, and shook the sistrum to please the gods.

Bes

Selket

Since ancient Egypt was a land of snakes and scorpions, the goddess Selket (or Serqet) was an important protector. She usually appears as a woman with a scorpion on her head, but sometimes as scorpion with a woman's head. Her name means "she who allows the throat to breathe," a reference to the fact that scorpion venom could restrict the throat and arrest breathing, causing death. Selket was believed to have power over all poisonous snakes, reptiles, and animals. Healers and magicians who treated people who had been bitten or stung invoked her power.

Because of her ability to release constrictions in the throat, Selket was reputed to have a role in beliefs about the Afterlife. She helped in the rebirth of the newly deceased person into his or her new existence in the Underworld by giving the person the breath of life. In burial tombs, Selket was a protector of the canopic jar (covered vase) that held the intestines of the mummified corpse.

Selket on a canopic shrine.

Heket

The Egyptian frog goddess Heket (or Heqet) protects all those concerned with childbirth—expectant mothers, midwives, and babies. She usually appears on temple walls as a woman with the head of a frog holding an ankh, though in amulets she is generally in animal form.

As the goddess of the last stages of childbirth, Heket is said to mold the child and its soul from clay, like a potter. Pregnant women often wore Heket amulets to protect them during the birth and Egyptian midwives called themselves servants of Heket.

In mythology, Heket is associated with the story of Isis and Osiris. It is said that she breathed life into the body of Horus at his birth. Like Osiris, she is associated with agricultural fertility, particularly with the germination of corn. The association of frogs with fertility and birth makes sense in ancient Egypt, where millions of frogs were hatched each year after the annual inundation of the Nile, which brought new life to barren fields.

Sekhmet and Bastet

Sekhmet and Bastet (or Bast) are the fierce and peaceful forms of the great feline goddess of Egypt. As Sekhmet, she appears as a woman dressed in red, the color of blood, with the head of a lion topped by a Sun disc and a cobra hood. As Bastet, she appears as a woman with a cat's head, surrounded by kittens, a sign of her motherly nature.

While Bastet is usually associated with the eastern rising Sun, Sekhmet is linked with the western setting Sun. Other texts give Bastet a lunar nature, while Sekhmet is a fiercely solar Lady of Flame, the fire-spitting eye of the Sun god Ra.

In myth, when Ra discovered that human beings were plotting against him, he asked the other gods for advice on how to punish them. The gods counseled that he send his divine eye to destroy humankind. Ra agreed and sent the raging lioness Sekhmet— world devourer and bloodthirsty warrior —to slaughter humanity. After Sekhmet had killed many people and waded in their blood, Ra had a change of heart. To distract Sekhmet from her orgy of killing, he asked his priests to dye jars of beer red and pour the beer on the ground. Thinking that the beer was blood, Sekhmet lapped it up and became too drunk to kill the rest of humankind.

Bastet is a goddess of love, fertility, and sensuality. Like Sekhmet, she is the daughter of Ra. In some images, she holds a sistrum as an emblem of festivals and intoxication. Worship of Bastet was centered in Bubastis in the Nile Delta region. In the 4th century BCE, the Greek historian Herodotus visited Bubastis and described a fertility festival held there in Bastet's honor. Worshippers arriving in boats sang, danced, feasted, and engaged in lovemaking. Excavations in the region have yielded many discoveries, including a graveyard where mummified holy cats were buried.

Bastet

Thoth

One of the most important gods in the Egyptian pantheon, Thoth is the god of wisdom and divine intellect. He appears in many forms, each of which conveys a different aspect of his being.

As a man with the head of an ibis (bird) wearing the crescent Moon and Moon disc, Thoth is the lord of time who measures the days and reckons the seasons. As an ibis-headed man with a scribe's palette and pen, he is the divine record-keeper and the inventor of the alphabet and the art of writing. As a baboon holding up the crescent Moon, he is the god of equilibrium who makes calculations, establishing order in the heavens and directs the motion of heavenly bodies. As a judge of the dead, he makes sure that the scales are balanced.

Thoth is also the god of magicians, physicians, and scribes. He is credited with writing 42 books of magic that explain the mysteries of the Universe. It is said that he taught Isis the words of power that allowed her to resurrect Osiris and was invoked by all those who sought to heal the sick. As the scribe of the gods, he is credited with authorship of all works of science, religion, philosophy, and every other branch of knowledge. Without his words, Egyptians believed, the gods themselves would not exist.

As a lunar deity, Thoth manifests as a baboon, which ancient Egyptians understood to be an intelligent, nocturnal creature that "sings" to the Moon at night. The curved beak of Thoth's ibis head also resembles the crescent Moon. Since its phases were easily observable, the Moon was important in Egyptian astronomy and astrology. Moon cycles were used to chart important civic and ritual events. For this reason, Thoth is credited with the invention of the calendar. He is said to have taken a part of each day of the lunar year to create the solar calendar of 365 days.

Thoth

Neith

The ancient creation goddess Neith has several manifestations. In the Delta city of Sais, she was honored as the patroness of weaving. Here, too, she was the mother of the mysteries of death and rebirth celebrated in the annual Festival of the Lamps described by Herodotus. In this aspect, she wears the shuttle of a loom on her head, holds the ankh, and weaves mummy cloths for the dead.

As the goddess of the hunt, she is patroness of warriors and hunters. In this aspect, she wears a set of crossed arrows on her head or carries a bow and arrows.

In her role as creation goddess, she is said to have spat her saliva into the primeval waters, out of which was born Apophis, the serpent demon who attacks the Sun at sunset and sunrise, smearing the sky with red. But Neith also reached into herself and drew forth the helpful frogs and fishes. The crocodile god Sobek is her son and she is also the sister of the goddess Isis (see page 305).

Khnum

An ancient creator god, Khnum was originally seen as the god of the source of the River Nile. In art, he often appears as a man with the head of a ram. The wave-like pattern of his ram's horns resembles the lapping waters of the Nile; one horn is the waters feeding northern Egypt and the other, the waters feeding the south.

On temple walls, Khnum sometimes holds a jar out of which flow the life-giving Nile waters. As the assistant of Hapi, the god of the Nile floods, Khnum makes sure that the right amount of silt is released into the water during the annual inundation.

From the dirt and silt of the Nile, Khnum models the bodies and souls of human children on his potter's wheel and places them in their mothers' wombs. In some texts, it is said that Heket, the frog-headed goddess (see page 309), is Khnum's consort. Her task is breathing life into Khnum's creations.

Wall painting depiction of Khnum.

Gods, heroes, and monsters in Greek and Roman myth

GREEK MYTHOLOGY WITH ITS HOST OF GODS, HEROES, AND
MONSTERS HAS SHAPED THE CULTURE OF THE WESTERN WORLD—
FROM ITS INFLUENCE ON ROMAN CULTURE AND RELIGION, THROUGH
THE GREAT REVIVAL OF ANCIENT CULTURE DURING THE RENAISSANCE
AND UP TO THE PRESENT DAY.

Greek influence spread not only through Greece and its islands, but also into Asia Minor (now Turkey), southern Italy, the northern coast of Africa, and the lands bordering the Aegean and Black seas. In time, Greek culture stretches back to the Bronze Age city-states of 1600–1100 BCE to the death of Alexander the Great in 332 BCE and the conquest of Greece by the Romans in about 146 BCE.

Every city or region had its own myths, heroes, and festivals. However, some story cycles were known throughout the Greek world. For instance, the supreme authority of Zeus, the king of the gods whose realm was Mount Olympus, was universal and unchallengeable. Perhaps the many tales told about the amorous adventures of Zeus reflect the desire for various regions to claim their particular god, goddess, or hero as a descendant of Zeus and thus bask in his power and authority. Similarly, the great Greek goddesses, such as Artemis, link Greek civilization to the early matriarchal cultures which are the world's heritage.

The epics

The epics of Homer were known throughout the Greek world. The events of the Trojan War (c.1190 BCE) and of the homeward voyage of the Greek war hero Odysseus, though not written down until

Ancient Greek vase depicting Medusa.

about 450 years later, were originally part of an oral tradition in which gods and kings, heroes, and monsters all played key roles. Similarly, the adventures of Herakles (also known today by his Roman name Hercules) were universally known. Shrines in his honor can be found throughout the Greek world. Though many of the sacred creatures described in this section are gods and goddesses, the coverage is by no means comprehensive. All of the sacred beings included here are connected in some way to mythic creatures. In some cases, their appearance links them to the fabulous beasts, such as the Hopi Kachinas of the American southwest. In others, the stories involve animal manifestations or transformations, such as the avatars of the Hindu god Vishnu. Other stories told here are the hero cycles in which a semi-divine figure battles a series of opponents, including many mythic creatures; the Labors of Hercules are one example.

In every case, these myths arise from the ability that most distinguishes human beings from other creatures: We are storytellers, the ones who tell the tales about all of the other creatures—including the gods.

Zeus and his consorts

Zeus, king of the Greek gods, had many consorts; some were goddesses and others were mortal women. Many of these couplings involved transformations; either Zeus became a creature to approach the object of his desire, or the woman was transformed as a result of her encounter with Zeus. Here are a few of the most famous.

Leda

To woo Leda, wife of King Tyndareus of Sparta, Zeus transformed himself into a swan that sought protection in her arms from a pursuing eagle. Once entwined, he impregnated the girl. Later that night, she lay with her husband. In due course, Leda gave birth to two eggs; from the first hatched the adventurers Castor and Pollux, who sailed with Jason on the quest for the Golden Fleece (see page 51); from the second, Helen and Clytemnestra.

Which of these children was mortal and which half-divine is not clear. Most traditions agree that Helen—who grows up to be the most beautiful woman in the ancient world and the cause of the Trojan War—was half-divine. Clytemnestra, likely a mortal, was the wife of Agamemnon, one of the leaders of the Greek forces in the Trojan War.

Europa

To win Europa, the beautiful daughter of Aegnor, Phoenician king of the city of Tyre (now in Lebanon), Zeus took the form of a great white bull. One day while Europa and her companions were picking flowers, a white bull appeared in the meadow. The beast was so beautiful and gentle that Europa was not afraid and caressed its flanks.

Lowering its head, the beast invited Europa to climb on to its back. When she did, the bull leaped into the sea and swam away, carrying Europa across the Mediterranean to the island of Crete. Once there, Zeus transformed himself into an eagle and coupled with the girl. Later, Europa married the Cretan king and among her children was the fabled King Minos, who imprisoned the Minotaur in the Labyrinth (see pages 81–83).

Italian vase painting depicting
Europa on the bull.

Danaë

To couple with Danaë, the daughter of Acrisius, king of Argos, Zeus transformed himself into a golden shower. Danaë had been locked in a bronze tower by her father because an oracle predicted that her son would kill the king. One night while the girl was lying in bed, she awoke to find herself bathed in a gentle golden rain. Soon, she discovered that she was pregnant and was delivered of a son whom she named Perseus.

When Acrisius discovered the child, he locked Danaë and her son in a chest and cast them into the sea. But the pair were washed ashore and after many adventures, including Perseus' rescue of Andromeda from the sea monster (see page 143) and his killing of the terrifying serpent-goddess Medusa (see pages 232–233), the oracle's prophecy is fulfilled. While taking part in games, Perseus throws a discus, which strikes and accidentally kills his grandfather.

Semele

Once when flying in the form of an eagle over the sacrifice of a bull in his honor, Zeus spies and falls in love with the priestess Semele, the daughter of Cadmus, the founder of Thebes. Disguising himself as a mortal man, Zeus becomes her lover and the couple conceive a child. Though he continues to visit her in mortal form, Zeus confides to Semele his true identity.

Hera, wife of Zeus and queen of the gods, discovers the affair and vows revenge. Transforming herself into an old crone, Hera persuades the girl to reveal her lover's name. Hera pretends not to believe Semele and convinces the girl to demand that Zeus come to her in his full magnificence. Reluctantly, Zeus agrees. Semele's intimate encounter with the god's lightning and thunderbolts burn her to a cinder. From the ashes, Zeus rescues Semele's unborn son Dionysos—Greek god of wine and ecstasy—and sews the baby into his thigh until he is ready to be born.

Roman mural painting of Danaë and two fishermen.

Callisto

Callisto is a nymph devoted to Artemis (see pages 324–325). Vowed to chastity, Callisto is a favorite companion of the goddess. Enflamed by Callisto's beauty, Zeus transforms himself into a likeness of Artemis. When the nymph lets down her guard, Zeus ravishes her.

Though Callisto tries to conceal her pregnancy from Artemis, when the nymphs are bathing with the goddess in a spring, Artemis discovers Callisto's condition and banishes her. Desolate, Callisto wanders off to have her child alone. Jealous Hera seizes this opportunity to take her revenge. She grabs Callisto by the hair and throws her to the ground, whereupon the Nymph is transformed into a bear.

Later, when her son Arcos, grown to manhood, is out hunting, he encounters the bear that was once his mother. Though Callisto tries to reveal her identity, Arcos aims an arrow at her. Taking pity on his former love, Zeus transforms the pair into constellations—Callisto becomes Ursa Major, the Great Bear, and her son Arcos becomes Ursa Minor, the Little Bear.

Io

Zeus also lusts after Io, a princess of Argos. To conceal this affair from his wife Hera, Zeus transforms himself into a cloud and the girl into a lovely white heifer. Suspecting her husband's treachery, Hera demands that the cow be given to her as a gift, a request Zeus cannot refuse. To keep her husband away, Hera asks Argus, a Giant with 100 eyes, to stand guard over Io.

Rescued by the messenger god Hermes, Io wanders the world, tormented by Hera who sends a gadfly to sting her wherever she goes. The western coast of Asia Minor, known as Ionia, bears her name because she ran down this coastline pursued by the gadfly. When she arrives in Egypt, Zeus restores Io to human form and she bears his child, who is the direct ancestor of Herakles (Hercules), the greatest Greek hero.

Io and Zeus

Artemis

Many of the Greek goddesses are associated with animals. A common symbol of Aphrodite, goddess of love, is the dove— statues of Aphrodite in Paphos, where one tradition says she was born, depict her holding a dove. Coins from Cyprus, also said to be her birthplace, are stamped with a dove. The emblem of bright-eyed Athena, goddess of wisdom, is the owl, which sees in the night.

But the goddess most closely connected to animal creatures is Artemis, daughter of Zeus and twin sister of Apollo, the god of the Sun. The oldest representations of Artemis (Diana in Rome) depict her as Potnia Theron, the Mistress of the Animals. One such image shows her with wings, grasping a stag and a panther (or lioness) by the neck. Another image that has been dated to 680 BCE shows her with a fish painted on her apron, surrounded by birds, a cow with crescent Moon-shaped horns, and a pair of ferocious lions. It shows that Artemis is the mistress of creatures of the air, land, and sea.

In later images, Artemis is most often pictured as a virgin huntress, barefoot or wearing hunting boots, with a bow and quiver of silver arrows. Though she is the goddess of the hunt, she is also the protector of all wild creatures. In some images, she is accompanied by a hunting dog or stag; in others she feeds a wild bird, such as a swan or a heron, from her hand. In a Homeric hymn in her honor, she is followed through the countryside by adoring wolves, lions, bears, and panthers.

As a fierce virgin, Artemis is very protective of her purity. When the hunter Actaeon accidentally comes upon her bathing naked with her Nymphs, Artemis is affronted. She transforms the young man into a stag and sets his own hunting dogs to chase him down and kill him.

Artemis

The Labors of Hercules

Hercules is the Roman name of the Greek hero Herakles. Because he is a son of Zeus by the mortal woman Alkmene, jealous Hera sends Hercules into a fit of madness during which he kills his wife and children. The Oracle of Delphi tells him that to atone he must serve Eurystheus, king of Tiryns. Eurystheus imposes 12 impossible tasks, many involving mythical creatures.

The Nemean Lion

This enormous and extremely ferocious lion that cannot be killed by an ordinary weapon is terrorizing the land around Nemea. When his bow and arrow prove ineffective, Hercules batters the lion with a club and then strangles it with his bare hands. To bring back its hide to Eurystheus, Hercules skins the beast with its own claws. The lion skin

Hydra

and the club become Hercules' emblems. The lion skin also makes Hercules invulnerable.

The Lernaean Hydra

The Hydra, a monster that lives in the swamps near the city of Lerna, has the body of a serpent and many heads—some accounts say nine, others, as many as a hundred. When Hercules slices off one head with his sword, two more grow back. To kill it, Hercules is helped by his nephew Iolus, who burns the neck of the beast with a torch when Hercules cuts off its head preventing it from growing back. Hercules dips his arrows in the Hydra's blood to make them poisonous.

The Cerynean Hind

This enormous deer, sacred to Artemis, goddess of the hunt, is larger than a bull, with bronze hooves and huge golden antlers. Named for Mount Cerynea, it is swift enough to outrun an arrow in flight. To capture it, Hercules chases the beast on foot for a year and then lames it when it stops to drink with an arrow from which the poison has been removed. After bringing it to Eurystheus, Hercules releases it so that it can return to Artemis.

Cerynean Hind

The Eurymanthean boar

This giant wild boar roams the land around Mount Eurymanthus, an area sacred to Artemis as Mistress of the Animals. With its razor-sharp tusks, it is ravaging farm fields in the highlands and terrifying the country people.

Ordered by Eurystheus to bring it back alive, Hercules travels to the region, where he is entertained by the Centaurs—half-men and half-horses. Urged by Hercules to open a cask of wine given to them by Dionysos, the Centaurs become drunk and attack Hercules, who defends himself by shooting them with his poisoned arrows. Only the immortal Centaur Chiron does not die. On Chiron's advice, Hercules drives the boar up the mountain into deep snow where he is able to subdue it and bring it back to Eurystheus. The king is so terrified by the giant beast that he hides in a jar—some say, a chamber pot—and orders Hercules to get rid of it.

The Augean stables

Next, Eurystheus orders Hercules to clean the stables where thousands of cattle belonging to King Augeus are housed. This magical livestock is immune to disease. Thus the amount of dung and filth built up over many years is enormous. To complete this task in a single day, Hercules diverts two rivers, the Alpheus and the Peneus, and causes them to flow through the stables, cleaning them instantly.

The Stymphalian birds

The Stymphalian birds are a flock of giant man-eating creatures with brass claws and sharp metallic feathers that they can shoot at their victims. Pets of Ares, god of war, they inhabit the region around Mount Stymphalia, where they destroy crops and fruit trees. To get rid of them, Hercules frightens them out of their hiding places with huge bronze clappers and then shoots them with his poisoned arrows.

Hercules and the Stymphalian birds

The Cretan bull

Eurystheus orders Hercules to capture the giant white bull that is wrecking havoc on the island of Crete and bring it back to Tiryns so that it can be sacrificed to Hera. Some sources say the bull is the one that kidnapped Europa; others that it is the bull with whom Pasiphae conceives the Minotaur. Hercules subdues the beast with his bare hands. But Hera, still angry with Hercules, refuses the sacrifice and the bull is released.

The mares of Diomedes

These four wild mares belong to the Giant Diomedes of Thrace, who feeds them human flesh. Hercules kills Diomedes with an axe and feeds his body to the mares, which makes them tame. Then he binds their mouths and leads them back to Eurystheus, who dedicates the horses to Hera.

The girdle of Hippolyte

Hippolyte, queen of the Amazons who are fierce female warriors, has a magic girdle (sash) that is coveted by Admete, the daughter of Eurystheus. Hera tells the Amazons that Hercules wishes to kidnap their queen. They attack and Hippolyte is killed. Hercules takes the girdle from her corpse. In another version of the myth, Hippolyte is so taken with Hercules' muscular physique that she gives him the girdle without a fight.

The cattle of Geryon

Geryon is a Giant with three bodies, three heads, six arms, and six legs. He guards his magnificent red cattle with the help of a two-headed watchdog. After killing the dog with his club, Hercules shoots the Giant in the forehead with a poisonous arrow and hacks his body into three pieces, then he herds the cattle to Eurystheus.

Cerberus

Finally, Hercules captures Cerberus, the monstrous hound of the Underworld, with three heads, the tail of a serpent, and a mane with the heads of various snakes (see pages 186–187). Using his bare hands, Hercules wrestles the monster into submission and drags him to Eurystheus.

Cerberus

Creatures of the Odyssey

The *Odyssey* (c.800–600 BCE) is the epic poem attributed to Homer (c.850–800 BCE) that describes the adventures of Odysseus (Ulysses to the Romans), a Greek hero of the Trojan War, on his long journey home to Ithaca after the fall of Troy. Many of these adventures involve encounters with mythical creatures, including the following:

Polyphemus

After a storm scatters the Greek fleet, Odysseus and his men arrive on the island of the Cyclopes—one-eyed Giants who live in caves. In search of supplies, Odysseus enters the cave of the Cyclops Polyphemus, son of the sea god Poseidon, who returns home with his flock of sheep to discover the intruders and eats several of Odysseus's men. The Giant blocks the entrance to the cave with a rock, trapping Odysseus and his men inside.

Clever Odysseus gets Polyphemus drunk on wine and blinds him by driving a pointed stake into his eye. Then Odysseus ties himself and his men to the bellies

of the sheep, and when the sightless Polyphemus lets the animals out of the cave in the morning, the Greeks escape. From his ship, Odysseus taunts Polyphemus, who replies by hurling huge boulders at the

ships. In revenge for the blinding of his son, Poseidon causes Odysseus to wander the seas for ten long years.

The Sirens

Later on his journey, Odysseus sails past the island of the Sirens, monsters with the bodies of birds and the heads of women, whose singing is so irresistible that it lures sailors to certain death. Following the instructions of the sorceress Circe, who has kept Odysseus and his men (whom she transformed into pigs for a time) enchanted on her island for a year, Odysseus tells his men to stuff their ears with beeswax and to tie him to the mast, so that they can keep rowing and he can listen to the Sirens' song.

Odysseus and a Siren depicted on a Greek vase.

Siren

Scylla and Charybdis

After passing the Sirens, Odysseus sails through a narrow strait—traditionally, the Strait of Messina between Italy and Sicily—each side of which is guarded by a monster. On one side is Scylla, a monster with six necks and six heads, each with gaping jaws and three rows of needle-sharp teeth. Below the waist, her body is made of growling dogs and a fish tail. On the other side is Charybdis, a whirlpool that is really the open mouth of a monster large enough to swallow a ship.

Scylla was once a sea Nymph (see pages 128–129), who was transformed into a monster by the enchantress Circe, jealous of the love the sea god Glaucus felt for the nymph. Charybdis was once a Naiad (see pages 128–129), daughter of the sea god Poseidon, who flooded the land to enlarge her father's kingdom. In revenge, Zeus transformed her into a sea monster whose unquenchable thirst causes her to swallow the sea, creating a whirlpool.

Polar opposites, Scylla stands for rationality; Charybdis, for mysticism. On the advice of Circe, Odysseus chooses to steer nearer to Scylla and loses only six men. But after arriving hungry on the island of Sun, Odysseus ignores Circe's warning and kills some of the cattle sacred to Helios, the god of the Sun. In revenge for this transgression, Zeus sends a terrible storm that destroys the ship. Clinging to a makeshift raft, Odysseus survives a second passage between Scylla and Charybdis. He grabs a fig tree that is growing from a rock and narrowly avoids being sucked into the whirlpool. At last he lands on the island of the goddess Calypso, where he spends seven years as the unwilling consort of the goddess.

Through the intervention of the goddess Athena, Odysseus is finally freed and returns to Ithaca, where he and his now grown son Telemachus battle the suitors who have been besieging his wife, Penelope. In the end, Odysseus is restored to his family and kingdom.

Scylla

Hindu and Buddhist sacred creatures

THE ICONOGRAPHY OF THE SACRED CREATURES OF INDIA, INDONESIA,
AND TIBET DIFFERS GREATLY FROM THE WESTERN OR EUROPEAN MODEL.
IN THE WEST, A CREATURE'S UGLINESS GENERALLY SIGNIFIES THAT IT HAS
AN EVIL NATURE. BUT IN HINDUISM AND BUDDHISM, TERRIFYING OR
WRATHFUL CREATURES, SUCH AS THE GODDESS KALI, OR CREATURES
THAT MANIFEST AS FIERCE ANIMALS, SUCH AS THE BARONG OF BALINESE
MYTHOLOGY, ARE OFTEN BENEVOLENT OR EVEN DIVINE.

The pattern for most Hindu and Buddhist mythological creatures began in India. The most ancient Hindu scriptures, called the Vedas, date back to at least 1500 BCE and were likely transmitted in oral form long before that date. The Vedas are a repository of mythological stories. Along with the great Hindu epics the *Mahabharata* and the *Ramayana*, they are the source for many mythic tales and creatures.

Hindu gods manifest in many forms. Rather than a single supreme being, Hindus venerate a pantheon of deities, many of which are considered to be manifestations of a central trinity called the Trimurti. The Trimurti consists of Brahma, whose role is creation; Vishnu, whose role is preservation and protection; and Shiva, whose role is destruction to clear the way for new creation. Though the various Hindu and Buddhist deities may seem to be distinct, underlying the differences is a sense that things are not what they seem and that all appearances are in some sense delusory. Thus Vishnu can appear in ten different forms, all of which share the basic purpose of maintaining the Cosmic order.

As Hinduism traveled to other lands and evolved new forms, it mixed with native mythological traditions. In Indonesia, tales and themes from the *Ramayana* are often presented alongside native mythological

Kali dancing upon the corpse of Shiva.

narratives in shadow puppet and dance performances. In Tibet, Buddhism, which originated in India, adapted elements of the native mythology to create a rich variety of sacred creatures. Even Tibet's native spirits became protectors of the Buddha's teachings.

338

Purusha and Prajapati

In Hindu philosophy, the world did not come into being through an act of divine creation, but rather as order arising out of chaos. Various mythic beings are used to describe this process.

One account from the earliest Vedas tells of Purusha, the "Cosmic man," a primeval Giant who is sacrificed by the Devas, or celestial beings. From Purusha's dismembered body, all the entities of the Universe come into being. Some descriptions say that Purusha has 1,000 heads and 1,000 feet. Other accounts say that Purusha's mind becomes the Moon, his eyes become the Sun and his breath becomes the wind. Other parts of Purusha's body become the Hindu gods. For instance, Indra, the chief god in the Vedas, and Agni, the god of fire, emerge from Purusha's mouth.

Human beings, it is said, also emerge from Purusha, according to the traditional Indian caste system. The caste of Brahmins (priests) comes from his mouth, the Kshatriyas (kings and warriors) from his arms, the Vaishyas (traders and merchants) from his thighs, and the Shudras (laborers) from his feet.

Lord of creatures

Another Vedic story tells of Prajapati, the "lord of creatures," a primeval Giant who emerges from a golden egg floating on the waters of chaos. Prajapati's first sound becomes the Earth and the next becomes the sky. After preparing himself through ascetic practices, Prajapati fuses elements of his own androgynous body, from which process the first beings are created. Among them is a daughter, the Dawn.

Desiring to mate with his daughter, Prajapati takes the form of a stag, while Dawn becomes a doe and runs away. As he pursues her, Prajapati spills his seed, from which the first human beings arise on Earth. In another version of the story, Prajapati actually mates with the Dawn in one animal form after another. From their union, pairs of all creatures arise, from human beings down to the smallest ants.

Purusha

The avatars of Vishnu

Vishnu, the Hindu god who is the "sustainer of the world," manifests as various animal and human figures, known as avatars or incarnations. They appear whenever the world is in danger.

Matsya the fish

King Manu rescues a small fish from the jaws of a larger one. The fish quickly grows to enormous size. Then Matsya reveals himself to be an incarnation of Vishnu; his blue-colored upper body with four arms appears from the mouth of the fish to warn the king that a world-destroying flood is coming. He instructs Manu to build an enormous boat and fill it with the seeds of all things and every type of animal. When the deluge comes, Matsya tows the boat to safety on Mount Himavan until a new era can begin.

Kurma the tortoise

At the time of the churning of the Ocean of Milk to recover *amrita*, the nectar of immortality (see page 94), Vishnu manifests as the tortoise Kurma. Usually depicted as the god Vishnu above the waist and a turtle below, Kurma supports Mount Mandara on his strong shell so that it can serve as a pivot for the churning.

Varaha the boar

When the demon Hiranyaksha steals the Earth and takes it to the bottom of the ocean, Vishnu manifests as Varaha, a being with a boar's head on a man's body. After battling the demon for 1,000 years and defeating it, Varaha carries the Earth out of the ocean between its tusks and restores it to its proper place in the Universe.

Narasimha the man-lion

Vishnu manifests as a being with a human torso and lower body and a lion-like face and claws to defeat the demon Hiranyakashipu, who is terrorizing the Universe. Since the demon cannot be killed by day or by night, by man or by god, Vishnu manifests as a half-man, half-lion and kills the demon at twilight.

Narasimha

Krishna

Vamana the Dwarf

Vishnu incarnates as a Dwarf to restore Indra's authority over the heavens, which was stolen by the demon Bali. Manifesting as a Dwarf with long hair, wearing a deerskin loincloth and carrying a water pot in one hand and an umbrella in the other, Vishnu asks Bali to grant him as much land as he can cover in three strides. When Bali agrees, Vishnu grows to giant size and strides from Heaven to Earth and from Earth to the lower worlds, thus winning back control of the Universe.

Rama

Vishnu also manifests as Prince Rama, the brave human hero of the Hindu epic, the *Ramayana*. Rama rescues his wife Sita, who has been kidnapped by the demon Ravana (see pages 163 and 216–217).

Parashurama

Another manifestation of Vishnu is Parashurama, a noble warrior whose name means "Rama with the axe," who rids the world of several evil kings who had become corrupt and arrogant because of their wealth and power. According to legend, Parashurama circles the Earth 21 times, killing the evil kings with his axe as if he was felling trees in the forest.

Krishna

The Hindu god Krishna is also considered to be an avatar of Vishnu. In images depicting his youth, Krishna appears as a young cowherd playing a flute. In the Hindu scripture the *Bhagavad Gita*, Krishna appears as a youthful prince who carries on a philosophical conversation with the warrior Arjuna prior to the start of a great battle.

Buddha

Hindus also consider the Buddha to be an avatar of Vishnu.

Kalki

This future avatar of Vishnu is a millennial figure who will appear when the current era of time draws to a close. Kalki is usually depicted as a warrior brandishing a sword in his right hand, riding on a white horse. He will cleanse the Earth of corruption, and renew righteousness and virtue.

Hanuman

Hanuman is one of the most important characters in the Hindu epic, the *Ramayana*. Hanuman is a Vanara—a human with the tail of a monkey. In Hindu mythology, these ape-like humanoids are said to inhabit the forests of south India.

Vanaras are brave, inquisitive, loyal, adventurous and kind. About 12 in. (30 cm) shorter than human beings, their bodies are covered with light brown hair, and they have monkey tails and simian faces.

Hanuman's birth

Several stories are told about Hanuman's birth. His mother Anjana is said to have been an Apsaras (see page 248)—a female spirit of the clouds and waters—who was born a Vanara as a result of a curse. The curse will be lifted when she gives birth to an avatar of the god Shiva. Hanuman's father is the wind god Vayu, who makes love to Anjana when she finishes her penance and Hanuman is the result.

As a young child, Hanuman thinks the Sun is a ripe fruit and flies up into the sky to catch and eat it. Indra strikes the child with his thunderbolt weapon and Hanuman falls to Earth unconscious, breaking his chin. Upset at this treatment of his son, Vayu withdraws all the winds from the world and living beings begin to die. Indra relents in his anger and the Devas revive Hanuman, granting him many powers. The cleft in Hanuman's chin is a permanent reminder of this incident.

In the *Ramayana*, a troop of Vanaras led by Hanuman is searching for Sita. When they reach the southern ocean, Hanuman remembers his powers and makes an extraordinary leap across the waters to the island of Lanka, where Sita is being held captive by the demon Ravana. Hanuman finds Sita and gives her a ring sent by Rama (see pages 216–217). Though Ravana sets fire to Hanuman's tail, he escapes to bring news to Rama and later fights bravely in the battle to rescue Sita.

Hanuman

Ganesha

Ganesha is one of the most venerated deities in India, honored by Jains and some Buddhists as well as by Hindus. He is called the "Lord of Beginnings" and the "Remover of Obstacles" and is recognized as the patron of arts and sciences.

Ganesha has the body of a human man, with a big belly, four arms, and an elephant's head, trunk, and single tusk. In some images, his lower right hand holds his broken tusk, while his lower left hand holds a dish of sweets. His upper hands hold various weapons, such as a noose, an axe, or a trident, which signify his ability to overcome obstacles. In some modern images, the lower right hand is turned toward the viewer in a gesture of fearlessness and protection.

Traditionally, Ganesha is the son of Shiva and his consort Parvati. In myth, Parvati creates the image of a human boy out of tumeric paste, brings him to life and asks him to stand guard over the house while she is taking a bath. Never having met his father, when Shiva returns, Ganesha confronts him. In the battle that ensues, Shiva cuts off Ganesha's human head with his trident and hurls it far away. When Parvati learns what has happened, she is distraught. Brahma suggests that Shiva replace Ganesha's missing head with that of an elephant. To devotees, Ganesha's elephant head symbolizes his intelligence and his large ears show that he listens to those who seek his aid.

The story of how Ganesha loses his tusk is told in the Hindu epic, the *Mahabharata*. The sage Vyasa asks Ganesha to act as his scribe as he dictates the poem. Ganesha agrees on the condition that Vyasa recite without pausing. While he is writing furiously, Ganesha's feather pen breaks; he continues by breaking off his own tusk and using it as a pen.

Ganesha

Kali

Her name means "the dark one" and Kali is a ferocious form of the Hindu Mother Goddess. In spite of her frightening appearance, Kali is considered by her devotees to be the kindest and most loving of the Hindu goddesses.

Each aspect of Kali's appearance conveys one of her attributes—she is black or dark blue in color. All other colors merge in black, signifying that Kali's nature is comprehensive and all embracing. She has angry red eyes, wild hair, fangs, and a long protruding tongue. But her wrath is directed solely against the forces that threaten order and harmony.

In some images, Kali has four arms. Her upper arms carry a sword and a severed head. The sword represents divine wisdom and the head represents the human ego, which must be cut away before a person can achieve liberation. Her lower hands carry a skull bowl that catches the blood dripping from the severed head, and a trident, the symbol of her consort Shiva. Kali wears a necklace of 50 human skulls and her skirt is made of severed human arms. The 50 skulls stand for the 50 letters of the Sanskrit alphabet, showing that Kali possesses all knowledge and wisdom. The arms represent the cause and effect mechanism of karma and show that Kali has transcended it.

Kali's emergence

In myth, Kali is born from the wrinkled brow of the goddess Durga (see page 78) during a battle against the demon Raktabija. Every drop of blood the demon sheds produces a duplicate demon and Durga is nearly overwhelmed. Kali enters the fray, brandishing her weapons and roaring with rage. She becomes so carried away that she begins dancing on the corpses of the slain. Among them is the seemingly lifeless body of Shiva, who appears under Kali's foot in many images. Shiva represents absolute, pure consciousness and Kali represents active creative power. Neither can exist without the other.

Kali

Sacred creatures of Bali

THOUGH HINDUISM IS THE PREDOMINANT RELIGION ON THE
INDONESIAN ISLAND OF BALI, BALINESE MYTHOLOGY COMBINES HINDU
STORIES WITH TALES, RITUALS, AND CUSTOMS THAT PREDATE THE
ADOPTION OF HINDUISM. THE SACRED CREATURES IN THE BALINESE
ACCOUNT OF THE CREATION OF THE WORLD AND ITS COSMOLOGY ARE
DRAWN FROM THIS TRADITIONAL MYTHOLOGY.

Bedawang

At the beginning of time, according to the myth, the only thing that exists is the world serpent Antaboga. Images of Antaboga, such as the shadow puppets used in traditional Balinese theatre performances, depict Antaboga with a Dragon-like head and a long serpent's tail. As a result of a period of meditation, Antaboga creates the world turtle Bedawang, who is often depicted holding up the Earth on its back.

On Bedawang's broad turtle back is a maze of coiled snakes and also the Black Stone, actually the lid of the cave that is the Underworld, where there is neither Sun nor Moon. The rulers of the Underworld are the goddess Setesuyara and the god Batara Kala. The Underworld is also the home of the great serpent Basuki. In Balinese culture, Bedawang is responsible for earthquakes, volcanoes, and other disturbances to the Earth's surface.

Batara Kala

This Balinese figure is the creator of light and also Mother Earth, over which there is a layer of water. Like Bedawang, Batara Kala is a god of the Underworld and rules over it from a cave in the company of the goddess Setesuyara. Shadow puppet images depict Batara Kala as a human figure with demonic features.

Above the Earth are a layered series of domes or skies. First is the middle sky.

Bedawang

Above that is the floating sky, the abode of Semara, the god of love. Above that is the dark blue sky with the Sun and Moon, and above that is the perfumed sky, filled with rare flowers. This is the abode of Tjak, a bird with a human face, the winged serpent Taksaka, and a group of snakes known as the Awan that appear as falling stars. The next sky is the flame-filled Heaven of the ancestors. The highest sky of all is the abode of the gods, ruled by Tintiya, the supreme deity.

Rangda and Barong

Rangda is a ferocious female folk demon in Balinese mythology. She is queen of the Leyaks—cannibalistic witches who practice black magic and feast on corpses. Her antagonist is Barong, a benevolent spirit king.

The conflict between Rangda and Barong is re-enacted by dancers wearing elaborate costumes and masks in traditional Balinese storytelling theatre performances. The masks worn by the dancers are considered sacred and are treated with great respect.

As portrayed in the dance, Rangda is frightening. She is a nearly naked old woman, with huge pendulous breasts, long white hair, and claw-like fingernails and toenails. Her masked face has bulging eyes, boar-like tusks, and a long, protruding tongue. The bulging eyes show that she is angry and cruel, the tusks that she is as merciless as a wild beast, and the tongue that she is always hungry for prey. During the dance, Rangda cries out in a shrill voice and emits terrifying grunts and shrieks.

Vengeful queen

According to legend, Rangda was once an 11th-century Balinese queen who was exiled from her husband's court for practicing black magic against his second wife. After the death of the king, the widowed queen—the word *rangda* means "widow"—takes revenge by bringing on a plague that kills half the population. She represents evil, black magic, and death.

Her antagonist Barong is a force for good. He manifests in the dance dramas as various mythic animals, such as a boar, a tiger, and a Dragon or serpent. In the region around the city of Ubud, Barong manifests as a lion. The Barong dancer's lion mask features a red face with an open mouth, surrounded by a mane of long, golden hair.

In the dance, Rangda casts a spell that causes the soldiers trying to destroy her to stab themselves with their poisoned spears, but Barong's counter-spell makes their bodies impervious to the darts. In the end, good triumphs and Rangda runs away.

Balinese carving of Rangda.

Tibet's wrathful protectors

The Dharmapalas are terrifying creatures charged with defending the precious teachings of Tibetan Buddhism. They are generally short, stout, and strong; some have multiple heads, hands, and feet, while others have three bulging eyes and metal fangs that drip blood.

Despite their frightening appearance, the Dharmapalas are embodiments of the Buddha's compassion, which can take an extremely wrathful form to help people overcome obstacles. Palden Lhamo and Mahakala are two such examples.

Palden Lhamo

This female protector is dark blue in color, with flaming red hair, symbolizing her wrathful nature, and wears a crown adorned with five human heads, symbolizing that she has overcome the five negative passions: anger, obsession, pride, jealousy, and ignorance. She rides side-saddle on a mule with an eye on its left rump.

In myth, Lhamo is married to Shinje, the king of Lanka, who practices human sacrifice and is an implacable enemy of the Buddha's teachings. Shinje has raised his son to do away with Buddhism in the kingdom. Lhamo kills the son and using his flayed skin as a saddle blanket, sets off for the north. Discovering Lhamo's flight, Shinje shoots her mount with an arrow, whereupon Lhama transforms the wound to an eye as a symbol of her vigilance in protecting the Buddha's teachings.

Mahakala

Blue-black in color, with six arms, Mahakala is a wrathful manifestation of the Buddha of Compassion. Mahakala's complexion—the color of the night sky—symbolizes the spaciousness of enlightened mind. His arms stand for his mastery of the six perfect activities: generosity, patience, morality, enthusiasm, concentration, and wisdom. His three eyes symbolize his knowledge of the past, present, and future. He wears a tiger skin representing the purification of desire and a snake for the purification of anger.

Mahakala, protector of Dharma

Sacred myths of China and Japan

CHINESE MYTHOLOGY CAN BE TRACED BACK NEARLY 4,000 YEARS.
THE EARLIEST LAYERS REFLECT TRIBAL SHAMANIC CULTURES THAT
WORSHIPPED MANY DIVINITIES, INCLUDING THE RAIN, RIVERS,
ANIMALS, AND HEAVENLY BODIES.

Chinese mythology

During the Han dynasty (202 BCE–220 CE) many early myths were rewritten as historical fact and dynasties were invented to account for mythic events. For instance, the early serpent-headed creator god Fu Xi was declared to have been the first of the mythical Five Emperors of antiquity. He ruled, it was said, from 2852 to 2737 BCE. Huang Di, another of these mythical emperors, was declared to be the ancestor of all Han Chinese.

China's two great indigenous spiritual traditions, Confucianism and Taoism, have coexisted for more than 2,000 years. Both have contributed to China's rich mythological heritage. Confucianism, which began about 500 BCE, puts emphasis on the family and on respect for elders.

These values gave rise to tales about household and ancestral spirits. Taoism, which was established by 100 BCE, seeks balance between two complementary and mutually dependent forces, yin and yang. Yang is masculine, active, light, hot, and dry. Yin is feminine, passive, dark, cold, and wet. In myth, the giant Pan Gu is credited with first differentiating these forces.

Shinto

The native religion of Japan, Shinto, honors the eight million gods and spirits of the invisible world, known collectively as Kami. Some Kami are natural forces, such as storms and earthquakes; others are features of the landscape, like mountains and rivers; still others are beings. Most of the Japanese mythical creatures in this

Huang Di

section fall into this category. However, around 500 CE, the first Buddhist missionaries reached Japan from Korea. Since that time, the Shinto faith has coexisted with Buddhism, leading to considerable mingling of the traditions.

Some Shinto Kami came to be considered opponents or protectors of the Buddha's teachings—for instance, the Tengu or bird-men. Other figures from Buddhism, such as the merciful Kannon, are regarded in some manifestations as similar to Kami.

Pan Gu

Among the accounts of the Creation in Chinese mythology is the tale of Pan Gu, a primal Giant similar to the Norse Ymir (see page 205). Pan Gu is usually depicted as primitive and hairy and in some images, he has horns on his head and wears furs. In images in modern shrines, Pan Gu is depicted as a stereotypical caveman, with long hair and a leopard-skin tunic. Sometimes he holds the Cosmic Egg, marked with the symbols for yin and yang.

According to myth, in the beginning nothing existed except formless chaos. The two vital principles of the Universe, yin and yang, come together to form a huge primordial egg, which grew undisturbed for 18,000 years. When yin and yang came into perfect balance, Pan Gu emerged from the egg, stood up and set about the task of creating the world.

With a swing of his giant axe, he separated the light and clear parts of the egg (yang) from the heavy and opaque parts (yin). Yang forms the heavens and yin forms the Earth. To keep Heaven and Earth separate, Pan Gu stands between them and holds up the sky for another 18,000 years until they solidify in their permanent positions.

In some versions of the myth, Pan Gu is helped in this task by four fabulous animals —the Turtle, the Unicorn (Ch'i lin), the Phoenix, and the Dragon.

Then Pan Gu lay down and died. His breath became the wind and clouds; his voice, the thunder; his left eye, the Sun; his right eye, the Moon; his hair and whiskers, the stars in the sky. His arms and legs become the four directions and four sacred mountains. From his body, mountains arise; from his blood come rivers; from his bones, minerals; from his marrow, diamonds; from his sweat, the rain. The wind carried the fleas from his fur all over the world and they became human beings.

Pan Gu

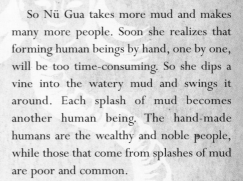

Nü Gua and Fu Xi

Another account of Creation in Chinese mythology tells of the primordial gods Nü Gua and Fu Xi. They are often depicted as a married couple, with human heads and torsos on the bodies of serpents; in some images, their serpent tails are intertwined. The serpent was the totem animal of the Xia, a tribal people who dominated China from about 2000 to 1500 BCE. This veneration of the serpent later developed into myths about the Dragon.

The story of how Nü Gua created the first humans is among China's oldest myths. Some time after the separation of Heaven and Earth, Nü Gua grows lonely, feeling that there is something missing in the world. After seeing her reflection in a pond, she scoops up a handful of mud and fashions the first human in her image.

When Nü Gua puts the creature down, it comes to life and wanders off.

So Nü Gua takes more mud and makes many more people. Soon she realizes that forming human beings by hand, one by one, will be too time-consuming. So she dips a vine into the watery mud and swings it around. Each splash of mud becomes another human being. The hand-made humans are the wealthy and noble people, while those that come from splashes of mud are poor and common.

Another version

According to another account, long ago Nü Gua and Fu Xi lived as sister and brother in the sacred mountains of Kunlun in the west. When two clouds of smoke they sent up into the sky intertwined, they understood that it was their duty to marry. Nü Gua created the human race out of yellow mud and Fu Xi became the first emperor. Fu Xi taught people to fish with nets and to raise domestic animals. He is also credited with devising the first musical instruments and inventing the first Chinese script.

Nü Gua and Fu Xi

Gong Gong and Zhu Rong

The water demon Gong Gong—an ugly monster with a snake's body and a human head covered with long red hair—is always striving to overthrow the order of the Cosmos. At this time, the ruler of the southern hemisphere is Gong Gong's father, the fire god Zhu Rong. In modern images, Zhu Rong is depicted as a warrior wielding a sword, clad in golden armor and riding a huge tiger.

Mustering all of the creatures of the sea and rivers, Gong Gong attacks his father Zhu Rong. But Gong Gong's troops cannot withstand the scorching heat of the Sun and he is defeated. Ashamed and enraged, Gong Gong smashes his head against the Imperfect Mountain—one of the pillars holding up the sky—causing it to collapse into a pile of rubble. As a result, a hole is torn in the heavens. The sky tilts toward the northwest and the Earth toward the southeast, which causes the rivers to flow southeast (into the Pacific Ocean) and great floods to inundate the land.

Moved by the suffering of the people she had created, the serpent goddess Nü Gua (see page 361) sets about repairing the damage. To fix the hole in the sky, she selects stones of five different colors from a riverbed and melts them in a furnace she has built. Then she flies up into the heavens and presses the molten rock into the hole until no cracks remain. To make sure that the repair holds firm, she kills a giant tortoise and uses its legs to support the four cardinal points of the heavens.

To stop the floods, Nü Gua burns rushes and uses the ashes to plug up the gaps in the riverbanks. Later, she teaches people the art of building dams and channels for irrigation. In some images, Nü Gua is shown holding a compass, which symbolizes her repair of the Earth's cardinal points, while Fu Xi holds a set square, which symbolizes the heavens.

Gong Gong

Houyi and Chang'e

Chang'e, the Chinese "Woman in the Moon," and her husband, Houyi, a celestial archer with magical powers, are featured in a well-known cosmological myth that dates back to the 6th century BCE.

According to the story, ten suns circled the Earth originally. The suns are brothers, and they take turns, each circling for one day. One day, all ten decide to circle the world at once. Crops wither and a terrible drought parches the land. The Jade Emperor, the ruler of Heaven, calls on Houyi for help. Houyi comes down to Earth, fits an arrow into his bow and shoots down one of the suns, which falls to Earth as a three-legged crow. One by one, he shoots down eight more suns, until only one remains. Pleased by his success, Houyi rids the world of other evils, including the Chimera Zha-Yu, the Minotaur Tao-Chi, and the winged Hydra Jiu-Yang, as well as a fearsome roc, a great python, and a giant boar.

Celestial selfishness

However, Houyi's wife, Chang'e, is unhappy. She longs for her home in Heaven and fears that she will die as a mortal and become a ghost. So she sends Houyi on a quest for the elixir of immortality. After an arduous journey, Houyi returns with the elixir. That night, Chang'e swallows all the elixir, reasoning that her husband is happy enough as a mortal.

Immediately, Chang'e floats up into the sky. Houyi cannot bear to shoot her down and so she flies to the Moon. She tries to call out, but she can only croak because she has turned into a toad. Her only companions on the Moon are a hare who is constantly pounding the elixir of immortality in a mortar and an old woodcutter who is trying in vain to chop down the Tree of Life.

Though she is restored to human form, Chang'e misses Houyi and realizes that it was a mistake to try to escape from mortal existence.

Chang'e

Huang Di

One of the mythical Five Emperors of China, Huang Di, also known as the Yellow Emperor, is honored as one of the founders of Taoism. He was a wise and benevolent ruler, and his long reign (2679–2598 BCE) was considered a golden age.

Legend says that Huang Di had four faces, which allowed him to see everything that was happening in the land. He rode around his kingdom in an ivory chariot pulled by Dragons and an elephant, accompanied by a procession of tigers, wolves, snakes, and Phoenixes.

Huang Di is venerated as a culture hero who taught his people the arts of writing, music, medicine, pottery-making, and the cultivation of silk worms. He also introduced the system of government and law. After ruling for many years, Huang Di grew tired and retired to a simple hut to practice meditation. At his death, he rose up into the heavens in the form of a Dragon and became a Xian, or Immortal.

Sun Wukong

Also known as the Monkey King, Sun Wukong is a mythical Chinese hero who accompanies the monk Xuanzang on a journey to India to bring the teachings of the Buddha back to China. His story is told in the Chinese epic novel *Journey to the West*, which was written during the Ming Dynasty (c.1590).

The Monkey King has many magical attributes. His main weapon is a staff banded with gold that can shrink down to the size of a needle so that it can be hidden behind his ear, as well as expand to gigantic size. He has fiery golden eyes and his monkey-shaped body is as strong as steel. He can travel vast distances in a single leap by performing a "cloud somersault" and transform hairs pulled from his body into duplicates of himself to help him in battle. When the mission is accomplished, Sun Wukong is granted Buddhahood for his strength and service.

Sun Wukong

Ryujin

Kami

Kami are spirits in the Shinto faith of Japan. The concept of Kami is very broad, reaching back into Japanese regional folk traditions and mythology. It is said that there are eight million Kami—"eight million" here implies an infinite number.

Some Kami are similar to the anthropomorphic gods and goddesses of Greece and Rome, such as the Sun goddess Amaterasu. Others are nature spirits and represent the vital energy of a mountain, tree, or river or of natural phenomena such as the wind, earthquakes, or storms. Still others are the spirits of ancestors, both royal ancestors such as the former emperors of Japan and the personal ancestors of every family. Each skill and occupation has a patron Kami, and the heroes of Japanese history are also often honored as Kami. Since many Kami are shape-shifters, some take the form of fabulous animals or have supernatural animals as their messengers or familiars. On the following pages are a few examples.

Ryujin

The Kami Ryujin is the Japanese Dragon god. In appearance, he is an enormous Dragon-shaped being, with a vast mouth and three claws on each foot, as is characteristic of Japanese dragons. Ryujin is often honored as the god of the sea or a personification of the power of the ocean.

He lives in a magical jeweled palace beneath the seas, built out of red and white coral. The palace servants are sea turtles, fish, and jellyfish. From this palace, Ryujin controls the tides using magical tide jewels —one jewel makes the sea rise and the other makes it fall.

However, as a shape-shifter, Ryūjin can also assume human form. He is the father of the beautiful goddess Otohime, who marries the mythological hero Prince Hoori, also known as Fireshade, a descendant of the Sun goddess Amaterasu. The grandson of this couple is the mythical first emperor of Japan, Jimmu-tenno. For this reason, Japanese emperors claim Kami as ancestors.

Earthquake Kami

Kami are traditionally believed to be responsible for earthquakes. The giant eel Jinshin-Uwo is so huge that the islands of Japan rest on its back. In the south, the city of Kyoto lies atop the eel's massive head. Aomori, 700 miles (1,126 km) to the north, lies atop its tail. In some versions, rather than an eel, Japan rests on the back of Jinshin-Namazu, a giant catfish.

To keep Japan from falling off the Kami's back, a rivet driven through a stone in the Shinto temple in Kashima called the *kaname ishi* or "keystone" secures the connection. But when the gigantic eel or catfish rolls over or lashes its tail, an earthquake or tsunami shakes the islands.

Similarly, the Kami Jinshin-Mushi— "earthquake beetle"—is a subterranean monster whose burrowing movements can also cause earthquakes. This beast is covered with scales and has the head of a Dragon and ten hairy legs ending in claws.

Inari

The Kami of agriculture, fertility and success, Inari is also a shape-shifter and can appear in many forms, both male and female. As a human, Inari may appear as an old man carrying rice or as a young female goddess.

In animal form, Inari most often appears as a pure white fox (Kitsune, see pages 224–225) but may also manifest as a snake, a Dragon, or even a spider. Foxes act as Inari's messengers, but may also be a mount for the Kami. Among the human-shaped manifestation of Onari is Dakiniten, a female Buddhist deity who rides through the sky on a flying white fox.

The entrance to an Inari shrine is usually guarded by a pair of white fox statues, often wearing red bibs. Devotees leave offerings of rice, sake (rice wine), tofu, and other food for these Kitsune messengers, in the hope that they will bring the worshipper's request to the attention of Inari.

Inari

Tengu

The supernatural creatures from Japanese folklore called Tengu, meaning "heavenly dogs," are sometimes worshipped as Shinto Kami. Tengu are usually depicted as kites or other birds of prey, but, even in bird form, they often have human characteristics. Their bird beak may become a long nose or they may have a human body with a bird's wings, head, or beak. As Kami, Tengu may take the form of beaked, winged figures with snakes wrapped around their limbs, riding on a fox.

Beginning in the 13th century, Tengu became associated with the Yamabushi, a religious sect that practices an austere mountain-dwelling lifestyle combining Shinto and Buddhist beliefs. Since that time, Tengu are often depicted in art wearing the small black cap and sash worn by members of this sect. In myth, the king of the Tengu is Sojobo, an ancient Yamabushi with long white hair and a long nose. He carries a magical fan made from seven feathers, showing his great power and strength. In legend, Sojobo's fan can be used to grow or shrink a person's nose, but also to stir up great winds.

Good and bad

The moral nature of Tengu is ambiguous and has changed over time. In the 12th and 13th centuries, Tengu were considered to be troublesome opponents of Japanese Buddhism. According to tales, they would pick up meditating monks and carry them to remote places and rob temples. But by the 17th century, Tengu began to be regarded as protectors of the Buddha's teachings. In one tale, a Tengu takes the form of a Yamabushi and becomes the personal attendant of the abbot of a Zen Buddhist monastery. When the abbot guesses its true nature, the Tengu's wings and huge nose reappear. After receiving a final teaching from the abbot, the Tengu departs, though it continues to watch over the monastery and to provide it with magical assistance.

Tengu rescuing Tameto from a giant fish.

Kannon

Among the most popular sacred beings in Japan is Kannon, a version of Guan-Yin (Kwan-Yin), the Chinese goddess of mercy and compassion. In Japan, Kannon is said to manifest in 33 different forms—one pure and sacred form called Shou Kannon and 32 manifestations suited to addressing the various needs of the people who seek help. Some of Kannon's forms are male and others are female. Some have multiple arms and multiple heads. Others are partly animal or ride on mythic beasts.

Among the most popular forms of Kannon is Senju Kannon, a male sacred being with 1,000 arms. Statues of Senju Kannon usually have two regular arms folded in prayer and 40 additional arms holding various implements. For instance, one of the arms holds a lasso that Kannon uses to catch devotees who need help, and then leads them to liberation. Each of the 40 arms stands for the 25 Buddhist worlds, giving a total of 1,000.

Other images show Kannon with ten additional heads as a headdress. One interpretation says that the multiple heads indicate that Kannon's mercy spreads in all directions. Another says that ten heads stand for ten steps on the path to enlightenment and the eleventh, the head of Amida Buddha, the Buddha of Japan's Pure Land Buddhist sect, stands for the goal of the path.

Animal forms

Batou Kannon is a manifestation in which Kannon's human head is topped by the head of a horse. In this form, Kannon protects horses and other farm animals. Stone statues of this form of Kannon were often placed in roadside shrines to protect riders from injury, similar in this role to a Shinto Kami. In other images, Kannon appears in female form riding on a giant carp or on a Dragon. Another popular female form, Koyasu Kannon, holds an infant and is said to help women have easy childbirth.

Senju Kannon

Sacred creatures of Native America and Mesoamerica

THE NATIVE PEOPLES OF NORTH AMERICA AND MESOAMERICA DEVELOPED
A WIDE RANGE OF CULTURES AND TRADITIONS THAT DEPENDED TO A
GREAT EXTENT ON THEIR LIFESTYLE AND ON THE GEOGRAPHY, PLANTS,
AND ANIMALS OF THE REGION WHERE THEY SETTLED.

In the Pacific Northwest, the Haida, Tlingit, and Kwakiutl peoples, for example, lived in coastal villages and enjoyed a mild climate and abundant food, especially salmon. Society was divided into clans, each of which honored a local animal as its totem (founder and protector). Images of beaver, eagle, and raven totems were carved on totem poles and other artifacts. The cultures of the Great Plains, such as the Cheyenne and the Lakota, told stories that grew out of their nomadic hunting lifestyle. The Lakota legend of White Buffalo Calf Woman reflects the importance of the buffalo to their survival.

The agrarian cultures of the desert southwest, such as the Navajo, Hopi, and Pueblo, and of the southeastern woodlands Cherokee, celebrated mythic creatures that assured agricultural abundance—examples include the Cherokee Corn Mother and the Kachinas who are said to have taught the Hopi ancestors new ways of farming.

Mesoamerica

Farther south, the native cultures of Mesoamerica—the civilizations of Central America and Mexico before the coming of the Spanish in the early 16th century —shared a cultural heritage that is surprisingly homogeneous. The Olmecs (c.1500–400 BCE), Maya (c.300–900 CE), Toltecs (c.900–1180 CE), and Aztecs (c.1100–1521 CE) shared a common sacred calendar based on their sophisticated astronomical observations and a style of sacred architecture consisting of enormous stepped stone temple pyramids.

The stories of their gods and mythic creatures, largely honoring heavenly bodies, wind, rain, and corn, as well as social phenomena such as war, are often interconnected among cultures and over a period of time. For instance, Quetzalcoatl, the Feathered Serpent, was honored as a creator god and culture hero by all Mesoamerican cultures.

Totem poles

Animal and Plant Creators

Many Native American myths give active roles in the creation of the world and the origin of people and their customs to figures representing sacred animals and plants. Generally, these creator figures are female.

Grandmother Turtle

According to a Cheyenne myth, in the beginning there is only the Great Water. Birds have no place to land and rest. So Turtle, the Earth Diver, swims down to the bottom of the primordial sea and retrieves a bit of mud. The mud begins to expand and becomes the first land. Soon there is so much land that only old Grandmother Turtle can carry it. To this day, the world is said to rest on the back of the Turtle, depicted in Native American art as a common turtle with sacred symbols decorating its shell.

Corn Mother

In a Cherokee creation myth the Corn Mother—sometimes depicted as a Native American woman with corn growing from her head—gives birth to two sons who are always hungry. Each day, she goes away and returns with a basket filled with corn. One day, the boys follow Corn Mother and watch as she scrapes corn kernels from her body. Because they have discovered her secret, Corn Mother tells her sons that they must drag her body through the fields so that corn will grow. Then she lies down and dies.

Spider Woman

A widespread myth among Native Americans of the western United States is that Spider Woman—depicted in modern images as a spider with the face of an elderly grandmother—weaves existence together like the strands of a great web. At the beginning of all things, Spider Woman spins lines of web that create the four directions. Then she makes people by molding them from various colors of clay—red, yellow, white, and black. Then she divided them into clans and gave each its totem animal. From these myths come the Native American belief in the interconnection of all things.

Modern painting of Spider Woman

White Buffalo Calf Woman

In addition to creating the world, sacred animal figures are also said to have given Native American peoples their rituals and traditions. In a Lakota myth, a supernatural female figure known as White Buffalo Calf Woman brings people the sacred buffalo, who gifts them with meat, hides, and other necessities of life, and the sacred pipe and other cultural traditions.

According to the story, in a time of famine, two Lakota hunters are scouting for food. In the distance, they see a mysterious and beautiful woman dressed in white buckskin. One of the hunters desires the woman and approaches her, despite his companion's warning. The hunter embraces the woman and is instantly reduced to a pile of bones. Then the woman approaches the other hunter and tells him to return to his people and prepare a feast for her arrival.

The hunter obeys and four days later a cloud comes down from the sky. Out of the cloud steps a white buffalo calf, which stands up and transforms into the beautiful woman, now carrying a sacred bundle in her hands. In the bundle is the sacred pipe, with a bowl of red stone representing Grandmother Earth, and a stem of wood representing everything that grows. Decorating the pipe are a carving of a buffalo calf representing the four-legged creatures of the Earth and 12 feathers from the Spotted Eagle representing the creatures of the air.

Then White Buffalo Calf Woman teaches the people how to smoke the pipe and to observe the seven sacred ceremonies, including the Sweat Lodge ritual for purification, the vision quest through which a warrior goes out alone to seek a sacred vision and the annual Sun Dance ceremony. Then she transforms again into a buffalo, bows to each of the four directions and disappears, vowing to return again one day.

Modern painting of White Buffalo Calf Woman

Coyote

Among the most popular and widespread Native American myths are tales of animal tricksters who use their cleverness to help people, entertain them with their clowning, and teach them valuable lessons. Trickster animals for various cultures include Raven, Rabbit, Mink, and Blue Jay.

Perhaps the most popular trickster in the stories of many Native American peoples is Coyote. He looks like a wild dog with fur, pointed ears, yellow eyes, claws, and a tail, but who speaks and acts in human ways. In nature, coyotes are known for their cunning. One of its tricks is to pretend to be dead to attract scavenger animals, which the coyote then catches and eats.

In one typical Navajo trickster story, Giants are roaming the world killing and eating people, especially children. One day, Coyote encounters one of these Giants and decides to teach him a lesson. He persuades the Giant to build a sweat lodge by promising that a sweat-bath will make the monster as agile as Coyote.

When the Giant and Coyote have entered the dark, steam-filled lodge,

Coyote tells the Giant that he will perform a miracle by breaking his own leg and healing it by magic to make it stronger. He takes a rock and uses it to break a deer leg he has hidden inside the lodge. Though he cannot see, the Giant can clearly hear the leg bone crack.

Modern painting of Navajo Coyote

Then Coyote sings a sacred chant and invites the Giant to feel his real leg, which is strong and unbroken.

Coyote offers to repeat the miracle on the Giant's leg. He pounds the Giant's leg with a rock until the bone cracks. He tells the Giant that to heal the leg, all he needs to do is spit on it. Though the Giant spits until his mouth is dry, his leg remains broken. Then Coyote slips out of the lodge and runs away, leaving the agonized and crippled Giant inside.

Kokopelli

Kokopelli is an ancient trickster god and fertility deity honored in many Native American cultures. He is usually depicted as a humpbacked flute player, with antenna-like horns on his head and, traditionally, an over-sized phallus.

The earliest images of Kokopelli on pottery and pictographs date to around 800 CE. Like many fertility gods, he is associated with agriculture and with the birth of game animals, as well as with human childbirth and sexuality. He is often pictured with four-legged animal companions, such as rams and deer, as well as with snakes and other lizards.

Many legends are associated with Kokopelli. In Ho-Chunk tales, his phallus is detachable and he sometimes leaves it in the river to impregnate young girls who bathe there. In Hopi belief, he carries unborn children in a sack on his back and brings them to women. As the god of agriculture, he chases away the winter with his flute-playing and brings the spring rains.

Thunderbird

A sacred bird in many Native American cultures, the Thunderbird is depicted in masks and carvings as multicolored, with curling horns and teeth within its beak. According to myth, Thunderbird is enormous in size; its wingspan is described as two canoe-lengths from wingtip to wingtip.

Each beat of these enormous wings pulls clouds together, creating thunderstorms, and lightning flashes are created by the blinks of the Thunderbird's eyes. Individual bolts of lightning are snakes that Thunderbird hurls to the ground from its powerful claws.

Cultures of the Pacific Northwest tell the story of Thunderbird and Whale. Whale is a monster who is killing other whales and depriving people of food and oil. Concerned that people are starving, Thunderbird flies over the ocean, swoops down and, after a fierce battle, picks up Whale in its powerful claws. The sound made by Whale dropping into the sea from a tremendous height is the source of thunder.

Thunderbird statue

Kachinas

In the Hopi and Pueblo cultures of the American southwest, Kachinas—meaning "life-bringer"—are supernatural beings that control various aspects of the natural world, such as rain, gourds, corn, animals, and heavenly bodies. Kachinas can also embody the spirits of dead ancestors. There are over 400 different Kachinas.

The home of the Kachinas, according to myth, is the San Francisco Peaks, a volcanic mountain range in north-central Arizona. Once during a great drought, the Hopis heard singing and dancing coming from these mountains. When they investigated the source of the music, they met the Kachinas, who returned with them to their villages and taught them new forms of agriculture as well as various rituals.

The Hopi believe that for six months of the year, the Kachinas remain with the people in their villages. During that time, ceremonial dances are held in which men wear elaborate costumes and masks representing various Kachinas. The costumes are considered sacred and the dancers are said to embody the Kachina during the dance. After the last ceremony called the Home Dance held in late July, the Kachinas return to the San Francisco Peaks. The annual visits of the Kachinas are believed to insure harmony in the villages as well as essential rainfall.

Kachinas are also important in Hopi initiation rituals. At age seven or eight, Hopi children are told the story of the Kachinas and are taught their ways and rituals. Young girls are traditionally gifted with Kachina dolls carved and decorated by their uncles during the springtime Bean Dance ceremony. One of the Kachinas in the Bean Dance is Crow Mother (Angwusnasomtaka). She is a female figure with crow's wings sprouting from the sides of her head. She wears a colorful skirt and carries yucca whips used in the initiation ritual and a basket of corn, symbolizing the start of the new growing season.

Wooden doll depicting Kachin Mana, a representation of the female sex in Kachinas.

Jaguar

The Olmecs, the earliest Mesoamerican culture, flourished in eastern Mexico between about 1500 and 400 BCE. Among their legacies to later cultures was a preoccupation with the Jaguar, which they linked with royalty, fertility, and sorcery. The largest big cat of the Americas, the Jaguar represented speed, power, and prowess in hunting and battle.

Mexican stone carving of a Jaguar.

Because Jaguar moves easily between worlds—they are equally at home in jungle foliage and lowland swamps and able to hunt both during the day and at night—the Jaguar was also the favored spirit companion (*nagual*) of the shamans. The role of these seers and sorcerers was to mediate between the human world and the world of the spirits. The Jaguar, they believed, could protect them on their "journeys" to the spirit world. Jaguar-shamans were especially feared because it was believed that they could magically transform into Jaguars.

In Olmec culture, Jaguars were depicted with a combination of human and animal traits. Archaeologists have termed these composite beings "were-jaguars" from the Old English word *were*, meaning "man" (see page 180). They range from human figures with a few jaguar features to kneeling figures that are more feline than human, featuring almond-shaped eyes, a snarling open mouth and a cleft running vertically on top of the head. Olmec figurines and ceremonial axe handles made of jade carved with the image of the were-jaguar are among the most recognizable artifacts of Olmec culture.

Among the Maya, the Jaguar was a fertility figure. Mayan kings wore Jaguar pelts, and many rulers took the name Jaguar, such as Jaguar Paw who ruled the city of Tikal in the 4th century.

Aztec versions

To the Aztecs, who based many aspects of their culture on the legacy of the Olmecs, the Jaguar was the symbol of their supreme god Tezcatlipoca, whose name means "Lord of the Smoking Mirror." Like the Jaguar, Tezcatlipoca was thought to be able to see in the dark and into people's hearts and minds. The Jaguar was also the totem of a society of Aztec warriors, who wore its spotted pelt into battle to signify that they, too, were fierce and aggressive.

Quetzalcoatl

This mythical hero, whose name Quetzalcoatl means "feathered serpent," is claimed as the common ancestor of almost all Mesoamerican peoples. He dates back to at least 200 BCE when representations of a rattlesnake with the long green feathers of the quetzal bird adorned the temple of the central Mexican city of Teotihuacan. In human form, he appears as a warrior adorned with feathers. A god of vegetation, rain, and wind, he was also linked to Venus, the morning star.

The founding king of the city of Tula, the capital of the Toltec culture (c.980–1168 CE), took the name Quetzalcoatl to elevate himself to godly status. The story of his exile from Tula likely combines actual historical details with mythic and religious symbolism.

According to the story, disputes arose between those who favored Quetzalcoatl—a priestly king who championed arts and culture and sacrificed only serpents, birds, and butterflies—and the followers of Tezcatlipoca—a Jaguar-shaman who demanded human sacrifice. Tezcatlipoca tricked Quetzalcoatl into getting drunk on fermented cactus juice. While he was drunk, Quetzalcoatl committed incest with his sister. Overcome with remorse, Quetzalcoatl exiled himself from Tula with a small band of followers.

There are several versions of what happened next. In one, Quetzalcoatl journeyed to the Gulf of Mexico, where he dressed in precious feather garments and a turquoise mask, set himself on fire, and rose from the funeral pyre as the morning star. Another has him setting sail on a raft of woven serpents, promising to return.

Yet another tradition says that because Quetzalcoatl thought that his face was ugly, he let his beard grow to cover it and eventually wore a white mask. This last version gave rise to the now discredited idea that the Aztec king Moctezumas opened his city to Spanish Conquistador Hernán Cortés because he believed that this bearded white man was Quetzalcoatl returning to his people as he had promised.

Quetzalcoatl

Coatlicue and Huitzilopochtli

The Aztec goddess Coatlicue is said to have given birth to the Moon and stars, while Huitzilopochtli is believed to have led the Aztecs from Aztlan in northwest Mexico on a great migration to their new home in the Valley of Mexico.

In Nahuatl, Coatlicue's name means "the one with the skirt of serpents." She appears as a woman wearing a skirt of writhing snakes. She has claws on her feet and hands and wears a necklace made of human hearts, hands, and skulls. A Mother Goddess, she presides over life, death, and rebirth, and is both the patron of women who die in childbirth and a monster who consumes everything that lives.

In myth, Coatlicue is impregnated magically by a ball of feathers that falls on her when she is sweeping a temple. Among her offspring is Huitzilopochtli—meaning "the hummingbird of the south"—the Aztec god of war and the Sun, and the principal deity of the great city of Tenochtitlan (modern-day Mexico City). In images, he has a black face, blue arms and legs, hummingbird feathers on his left leg, feather-tipped arrows, and a spear-thrower in the shape of a serpent.

A solar god

Like Quetzalcoatl, Huitzilopochtli is regarded as a culture hero. The Aztecs believed that he led them to their new home in the Valley of Mexico. The sign that they had arrived at the right place was an eagle perched on a cactus eating a snake—the image that now appears on the Mexican flag. Huitzilopochtli promised that once established in their new capital, the Aztecs would become the masters of the known world and conquered nations would bring them tribute of gold, precious stones, and quetzal feathers. As a solar god, Huitzilopochtli was engaged in a constant struggle with the darkness and required nourishment in the form of sacrifices in order to survive. Aztec warriors who died on the sacrificial altar were believed to form part of the Sun's retinue for four years, after which they lived forever inside the bodies of hummingbirds.

Huitzilopochtli

Index

Acknowledgments

Aberdeen University 25. **AISA Media** 249. **akg-images** 29, 189, Erich Lessing 232, 304, 319, 320. **Alamy** J Marshall/Tribaleye Images 352, Sherab 355. **Ancient Art & Architecture Collection** 297, 317, 332, 372, 377, 389. **The Bridgeman Art Library** Atkinson Art Gallery, Southport 295, Archives Charmet/Private Collection 235, Collection of the Earl of Leicester, Holkham Hall, Norfolk 171, The Detroit Institute of Arts, USA, Founders Society Purchase 65, Dreamtime Gallery, London 66, Egyptian National Museum/Boltin Picture Library 308, Galleria degli Uffizi, Florence, Italy 125, Hamburger Kunsthalle, Germany 57, Kunsthaus Zurich, Switzerland 263, Nationalmuseum, Stockholm, Sweden 214, Peter Newark Western Americana/Private Collection 385, Roy Miles Fine Paintings 291, Whitford & Hughes, London 198. **China Tourism Photo Library** 357. **Corbis** Araldo de Luca 154, Blue Lantern Studio 161, Christie's Images 158, Francis G Mayer 71, Historical Picture Archive 293, Phillipe Lissac/Godong 337, Sandro Vannini 175. **iStock** Duncan Walker 54. **Mary Evans Picture Library** 19, 49, 207, 209, 282, Rue des Archives 393.

National Museum of the American Indian, Smithsonian Institution 383. **Rogue Guirey Simpson Estate** 381. **Scala** Bildarchiv Preussischer Kulturbesitz, Berlin 180, CM Dixon/HIP 315, The Philadelphia Museum of Art/Art Resource 79. **Susan St Thomas** www.sttomasstudio.com 379. **TopFoto.co.uk** 95, Ancient Art & Architecture Collection 115. **Werner Forman** Archive British Museum 281, Christie's London 82, Museum fur Volkerkunde, Berlin 390, Private collection 61, 72, 74–5. **Wikipedia** 88, 101, Marie-Lan Nguyen 86.

Executive Editor Sandra Rigby
Managing Editors Clare Churly and Camilla Davis
Executive Art Editor Sally Bond
Designer Rebecca Johns at Cobalt id
Illustrators Dean Spencer, John Higgins and John Davis
Picture Researchers Roland and Sarah Smithies
Production Controller Hannah Burke